LETTER TRACING

PRACTICE WORKBOOK

FOR PRESCHOOLERS

COPYRIGHT NOTICE

Copyright © 2017 by Christine Joy

A

airplane   astronaut

apple   ant

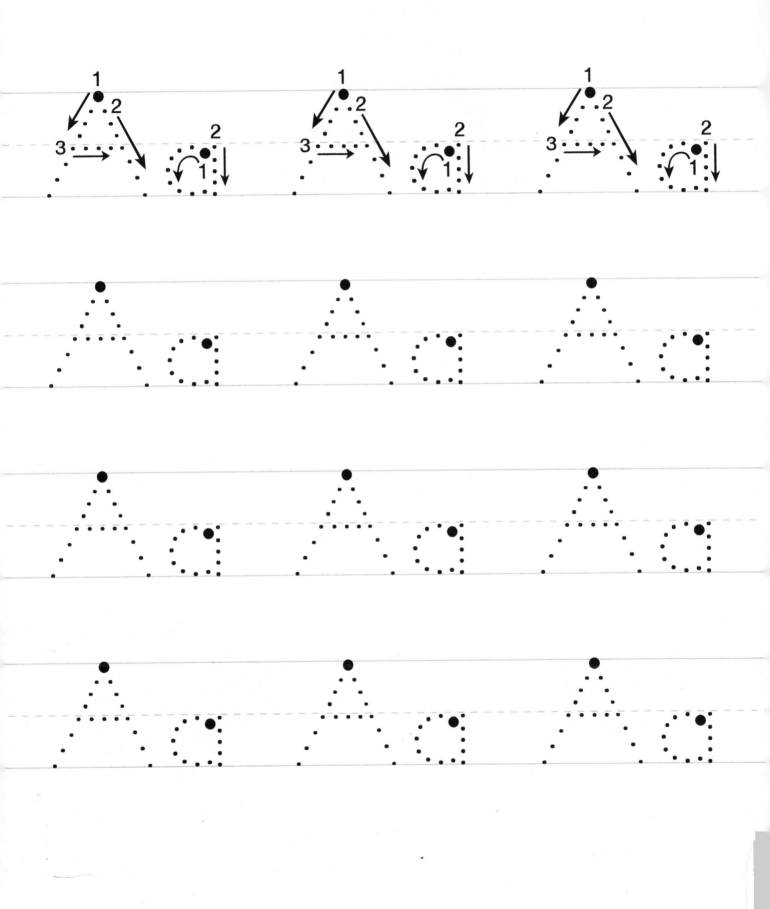

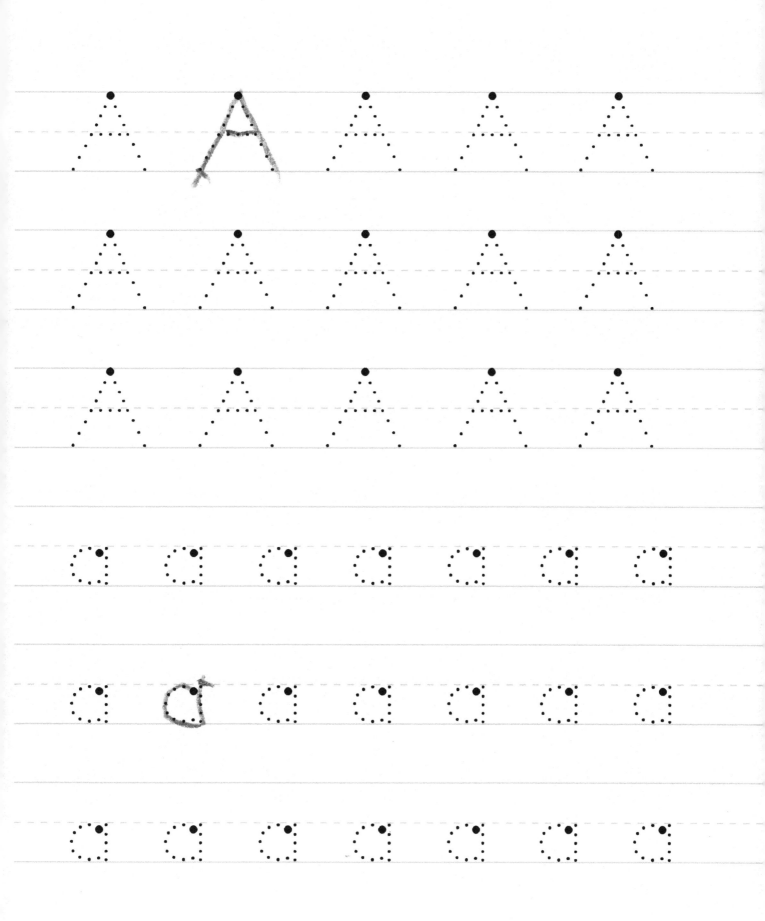

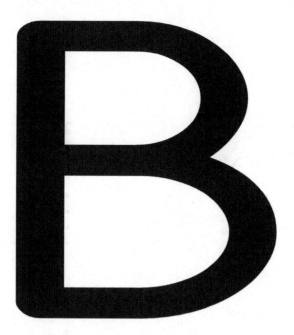

B

banana

bike

bus

ball

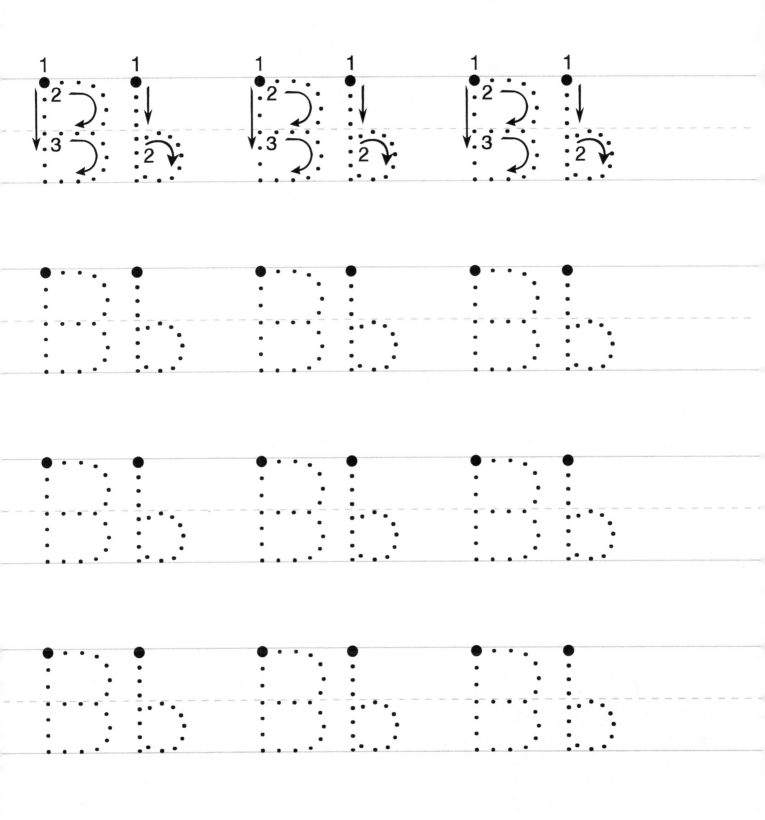

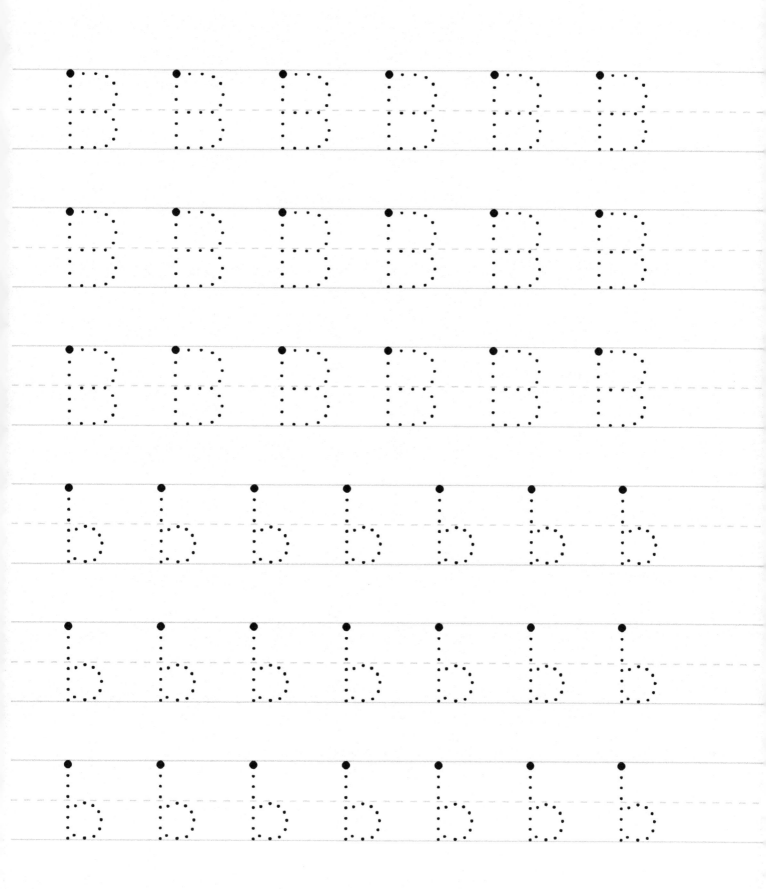

C

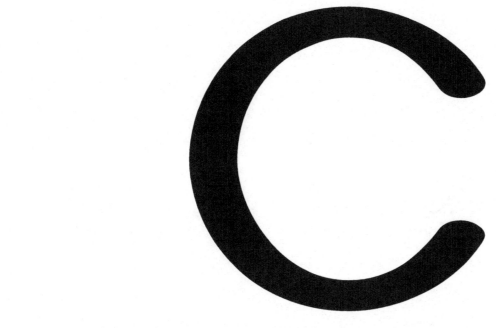

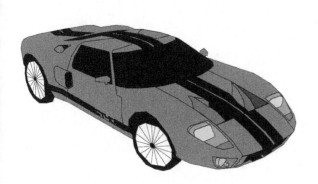

car

corn

caterpillar

cat

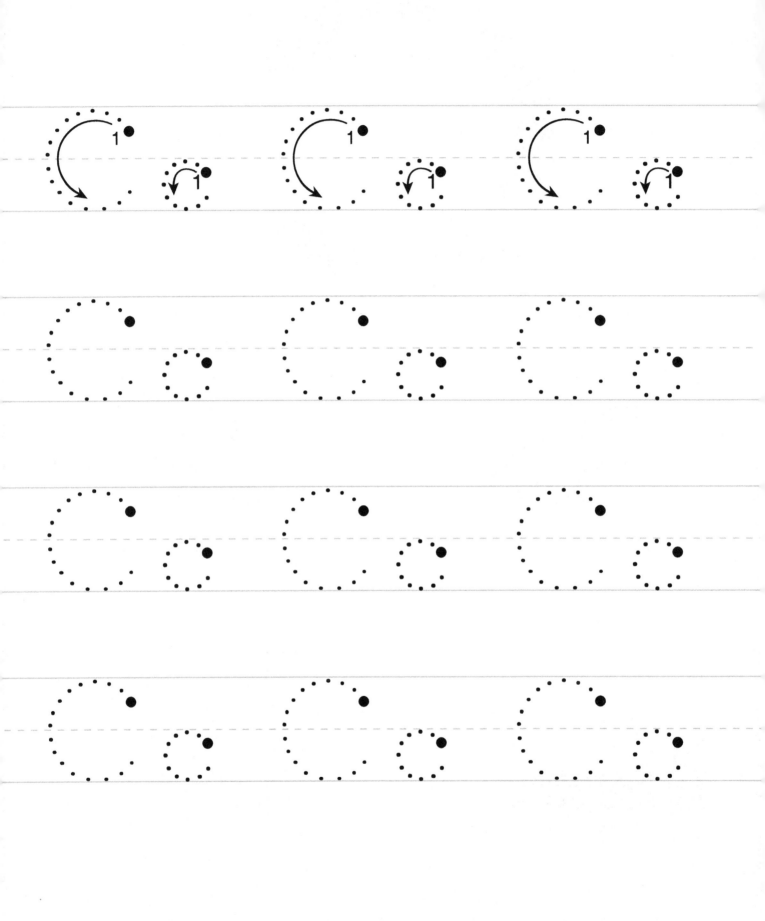

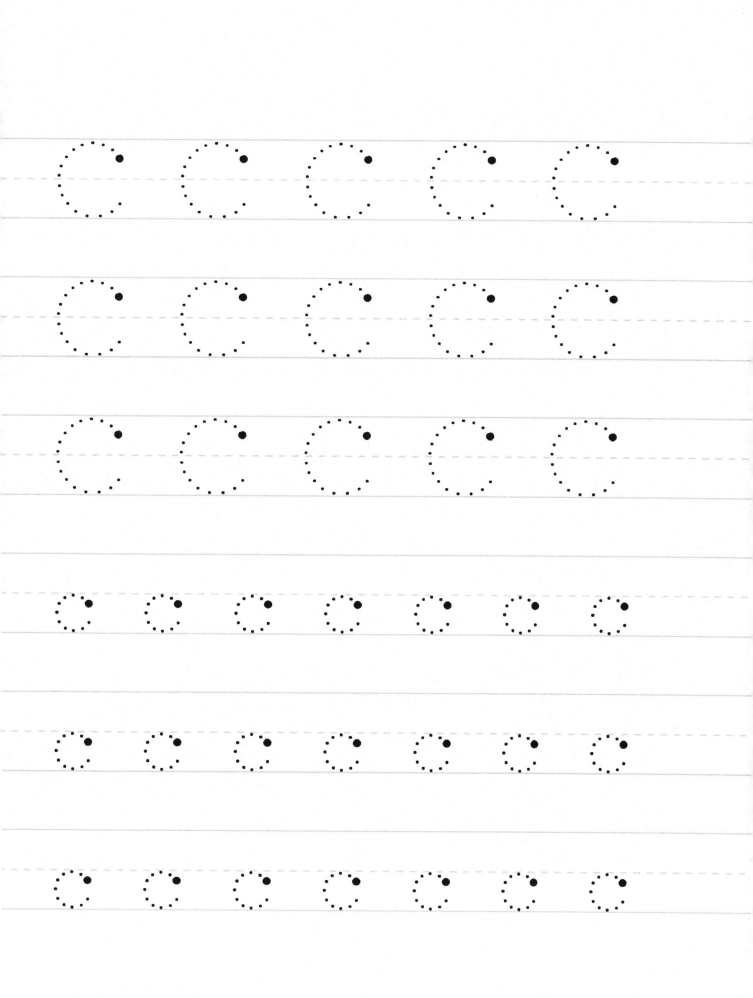

D

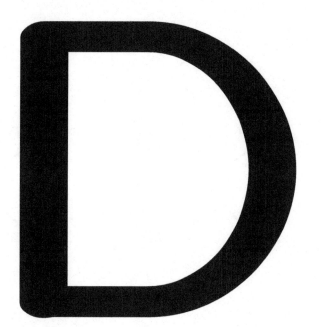

deer

drum

donkey

dog

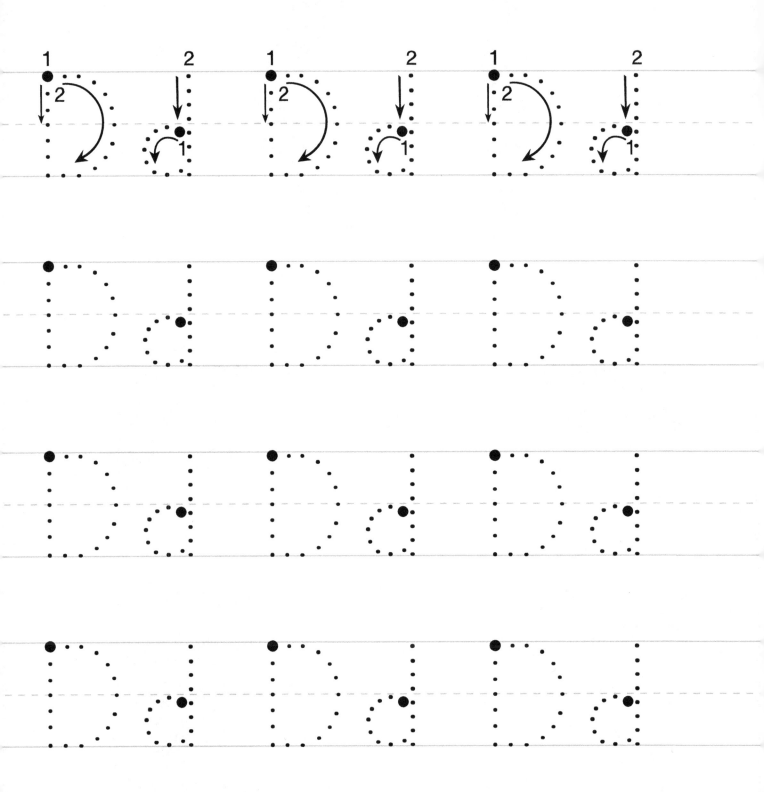

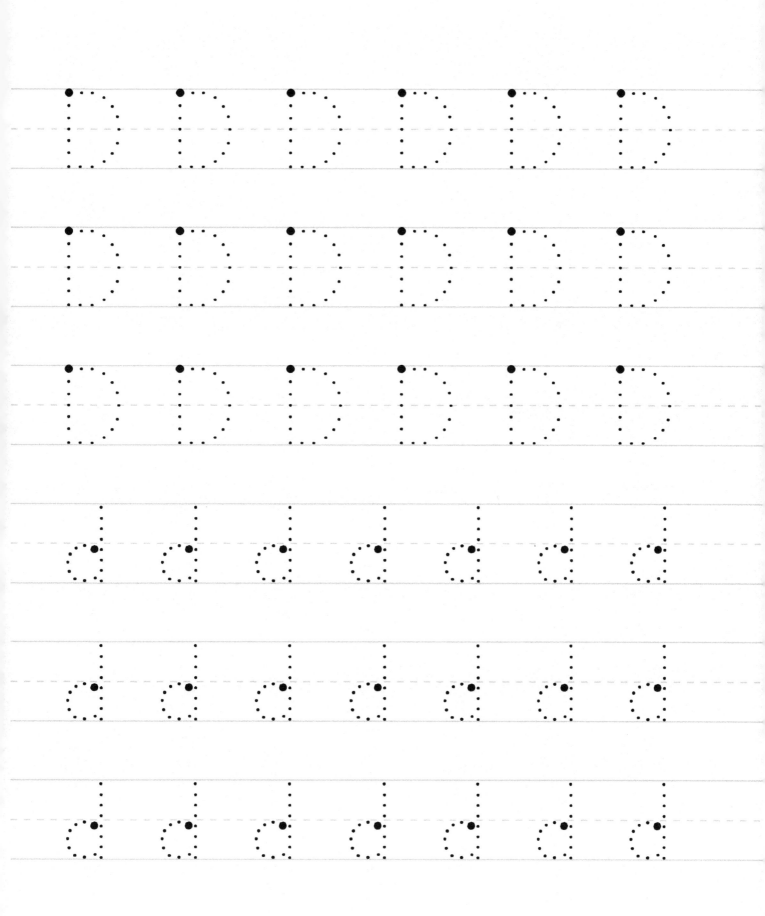

E

egg

envelope

elephant

eggplant

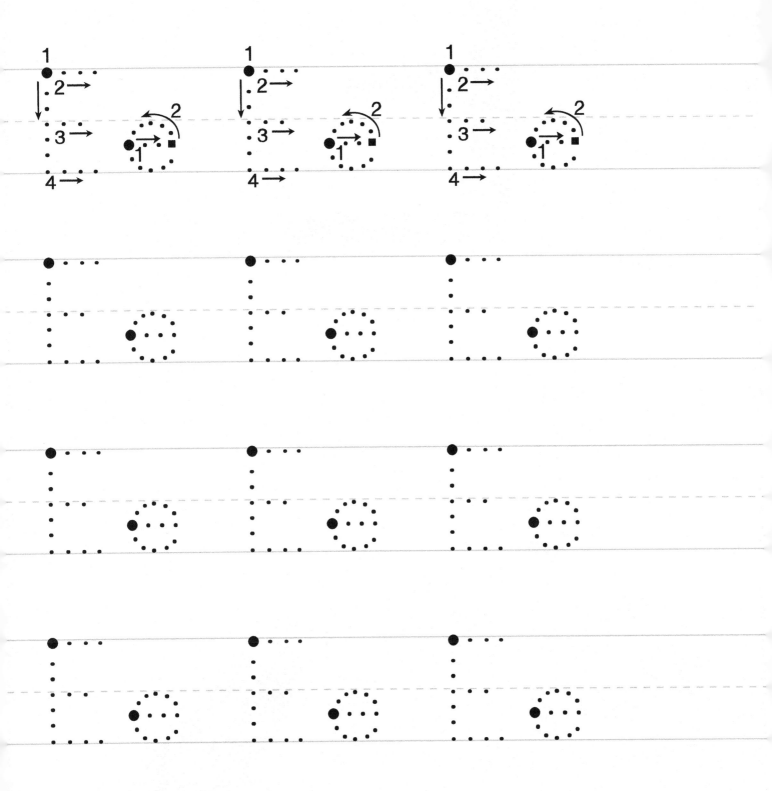

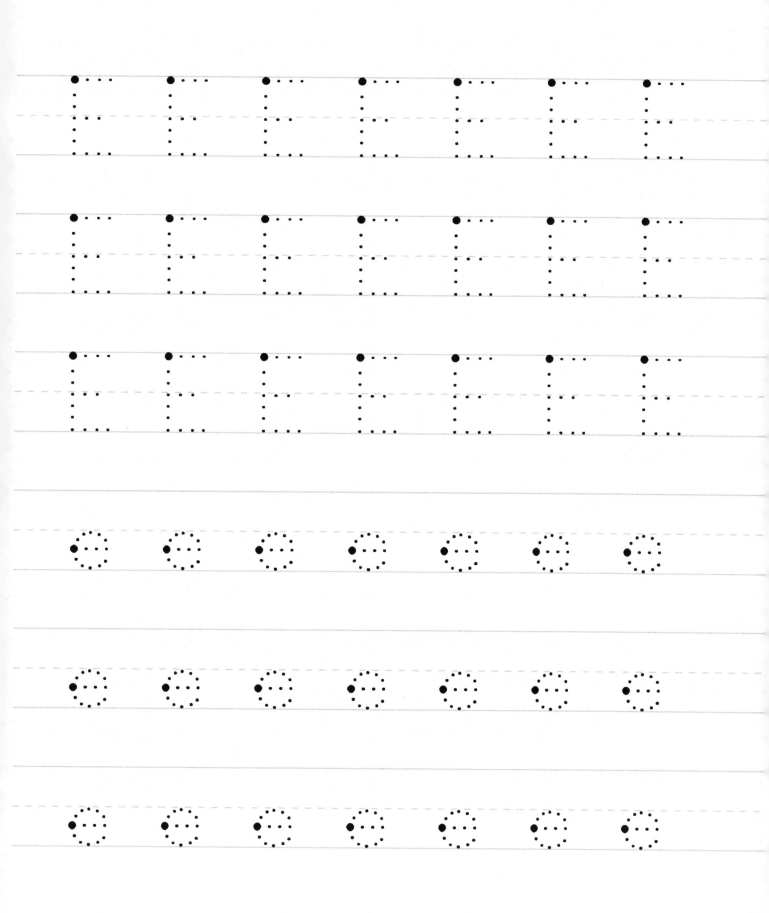

F

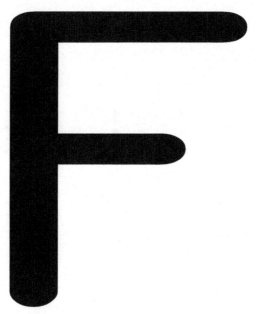

fish

flower

frog

flamingo

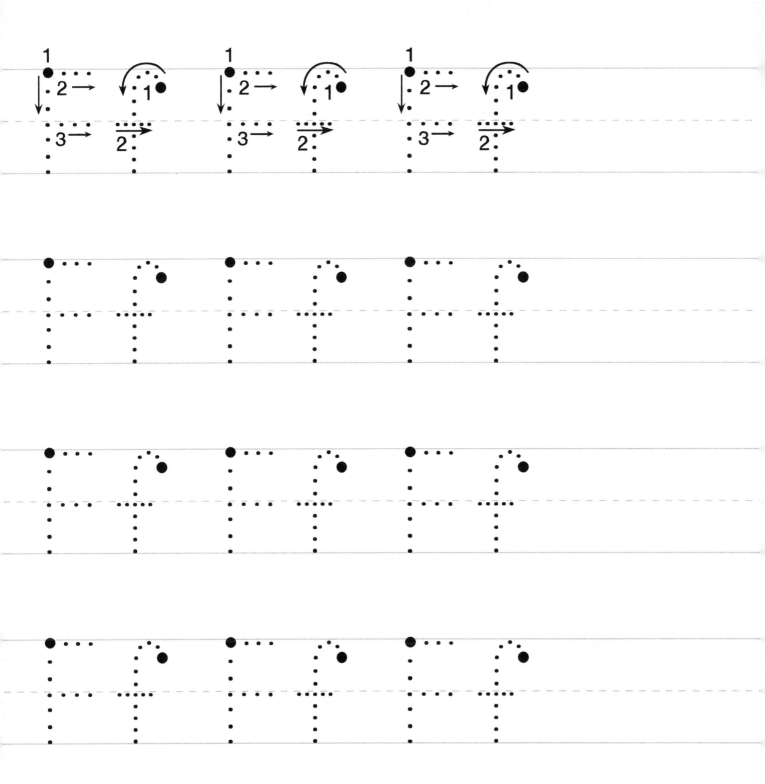

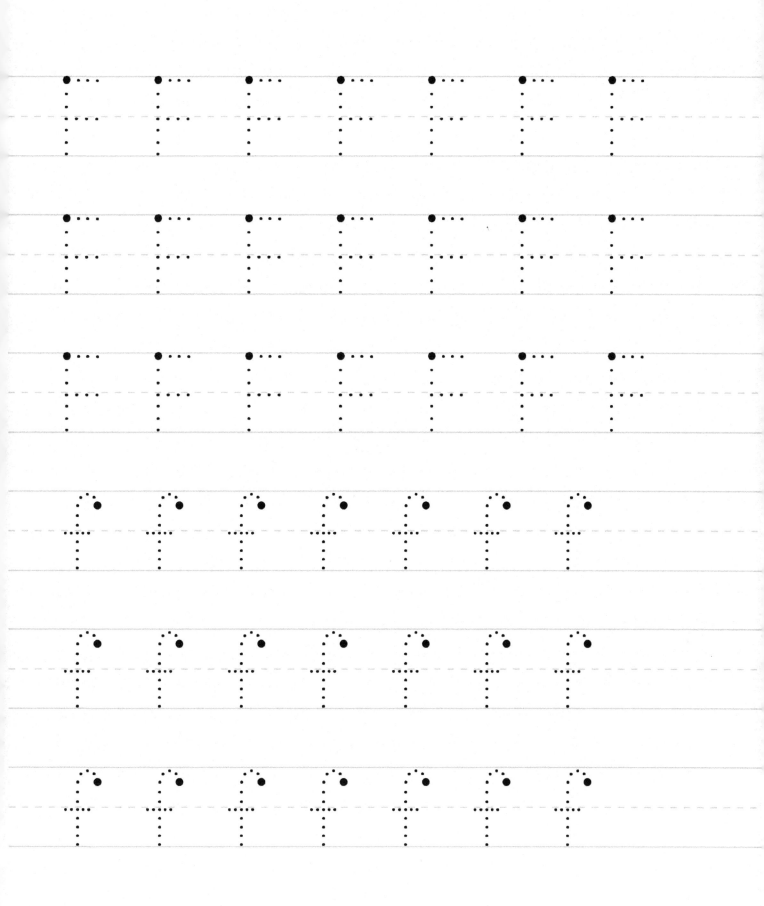

G

gift

gorilla

goose

giraffe

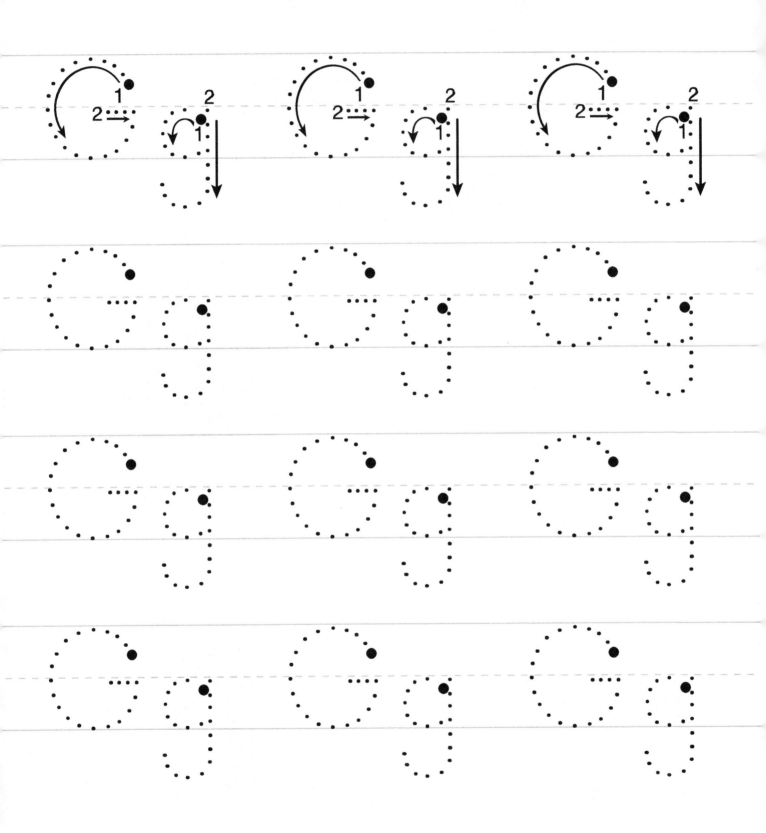

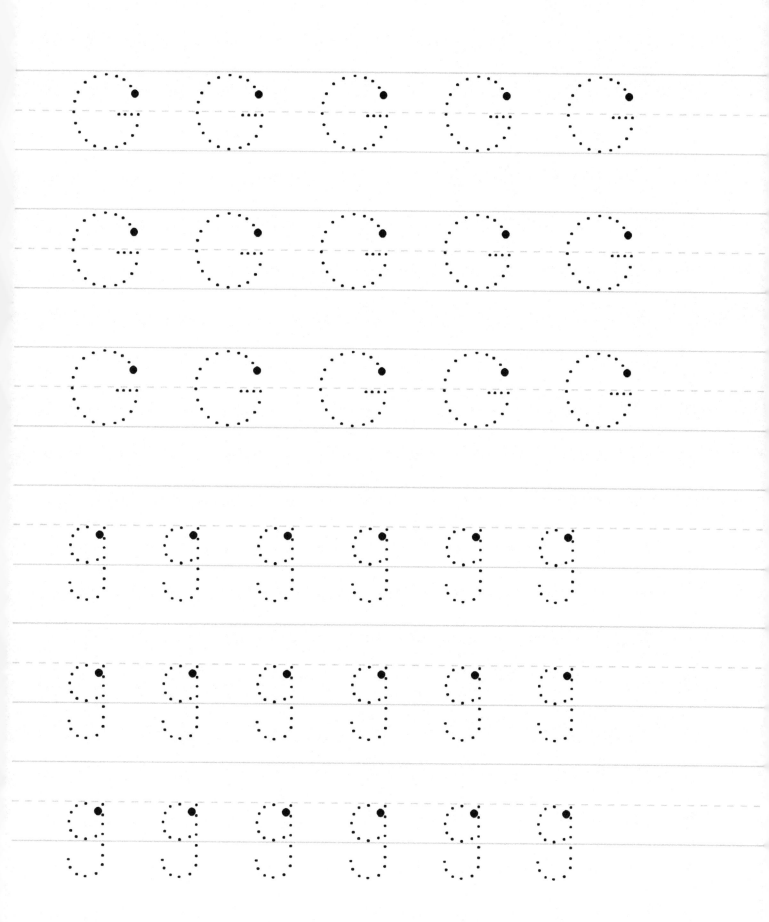

H

hammer

horse

hat

hippo

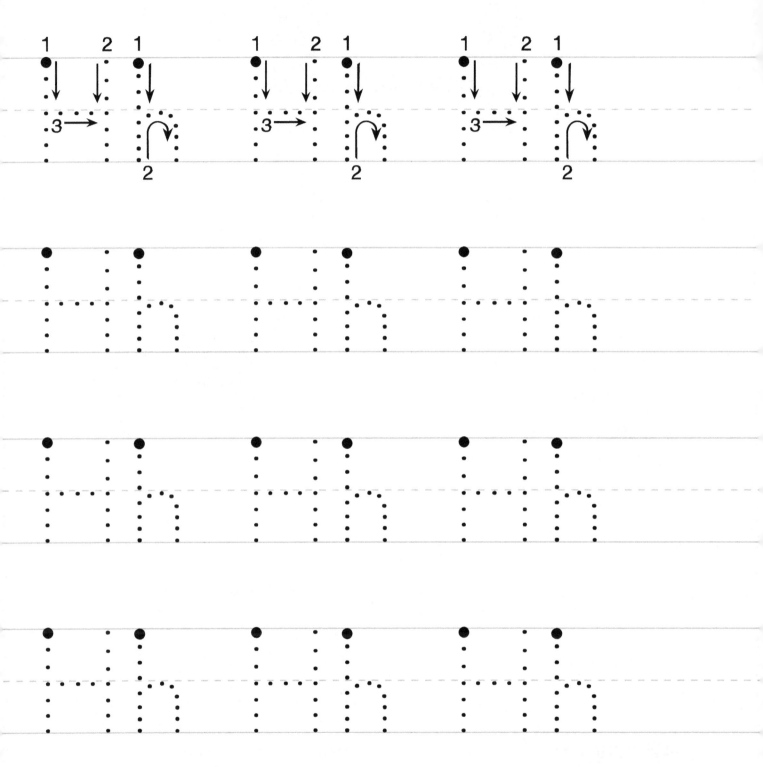

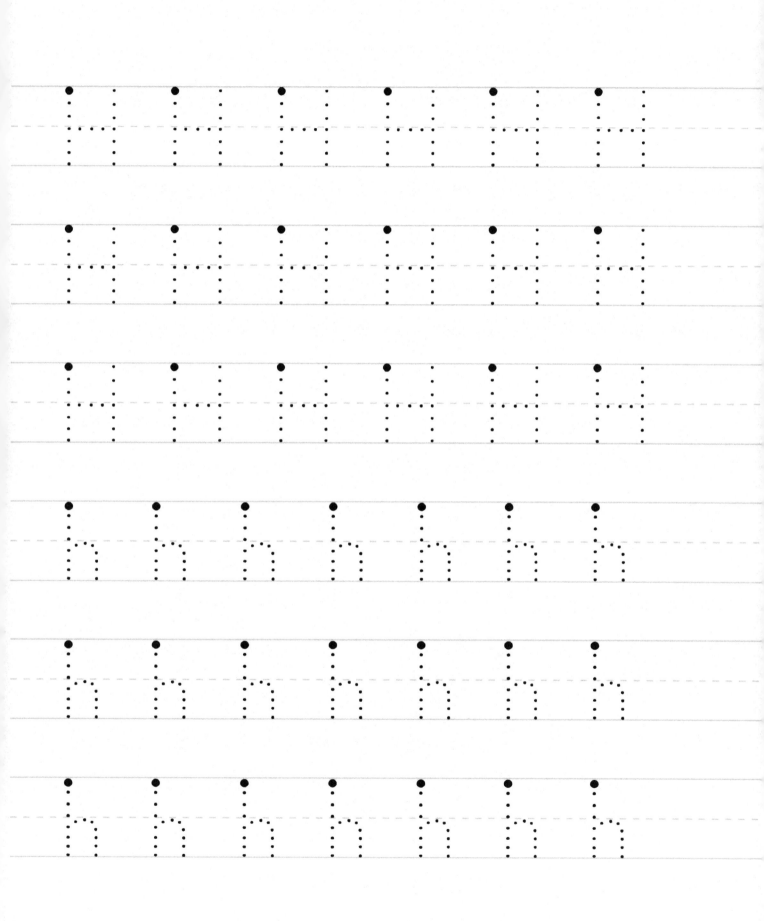

I

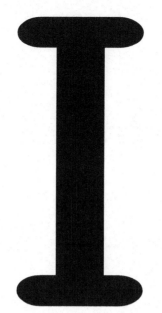

island

ice cream

iguana

igloo

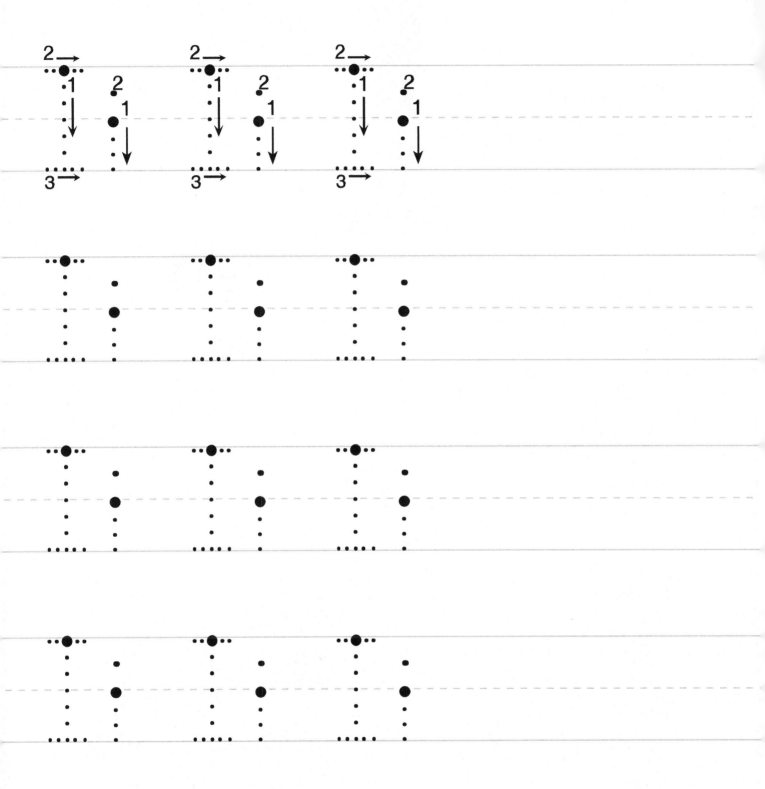

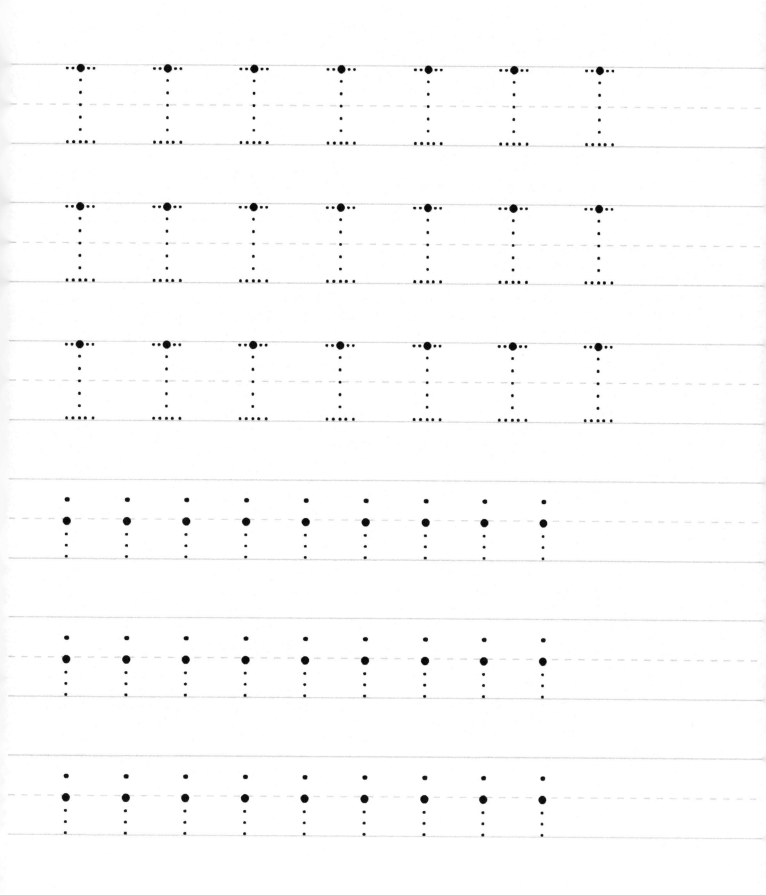

J

jacket

juice

jet

jar

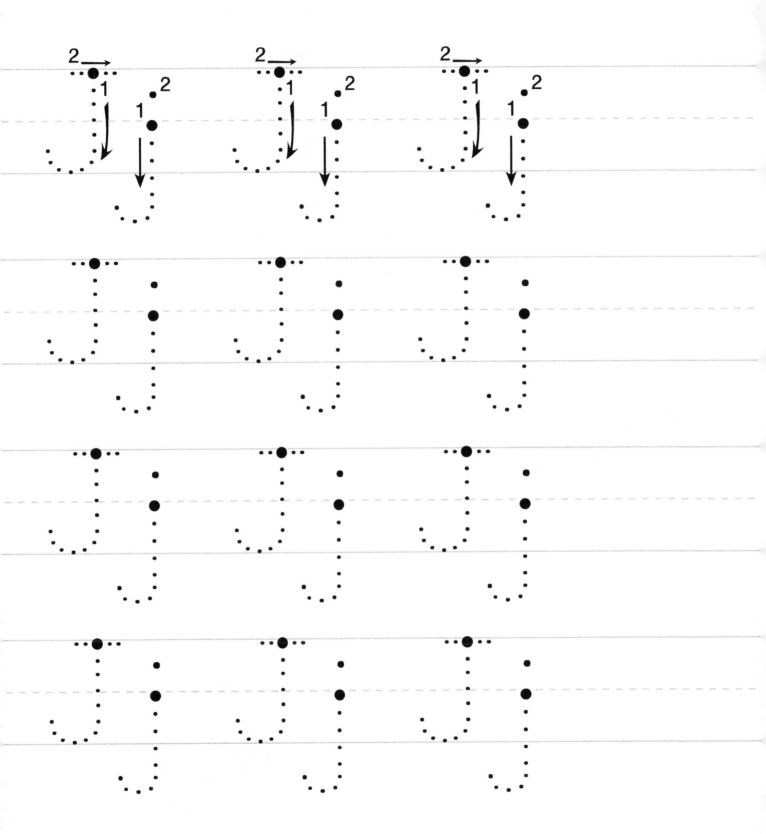

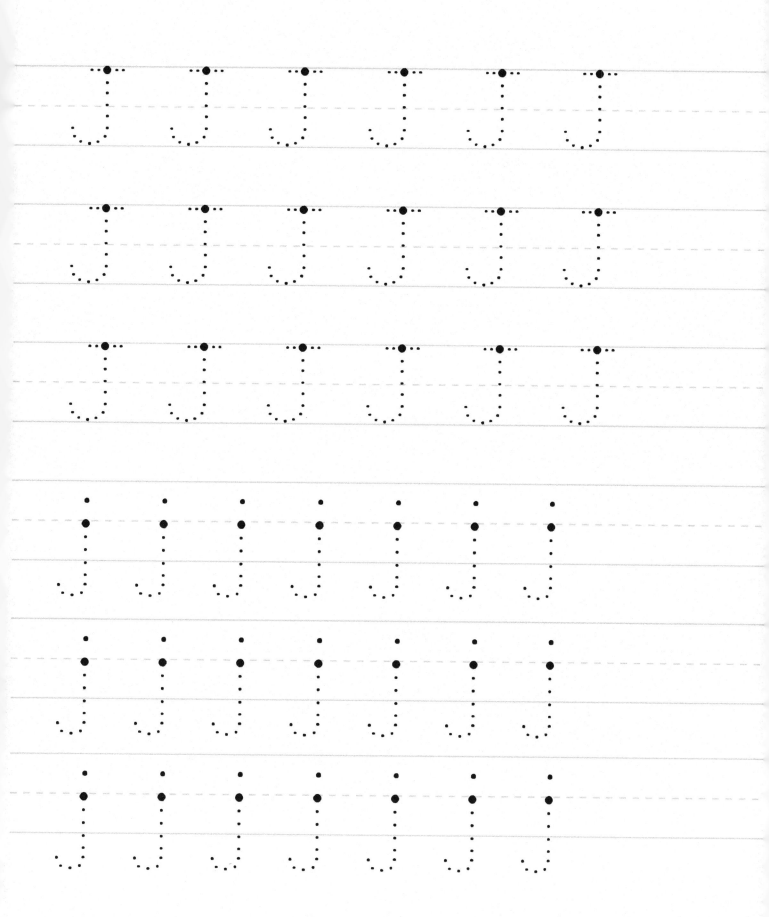

K

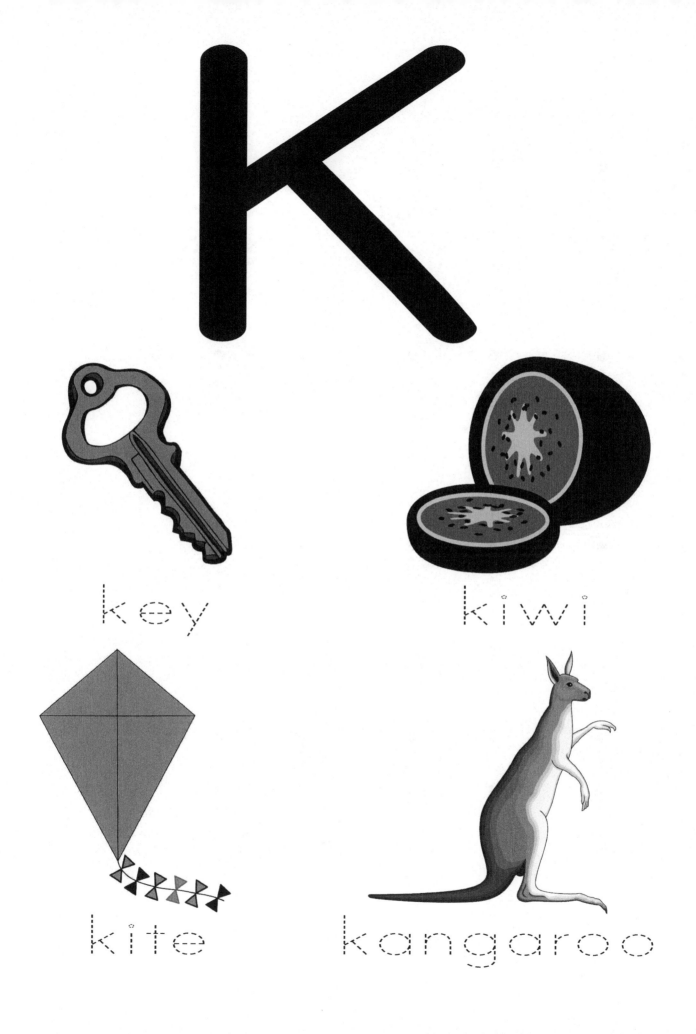

key

kiwi

kite

kangaroo

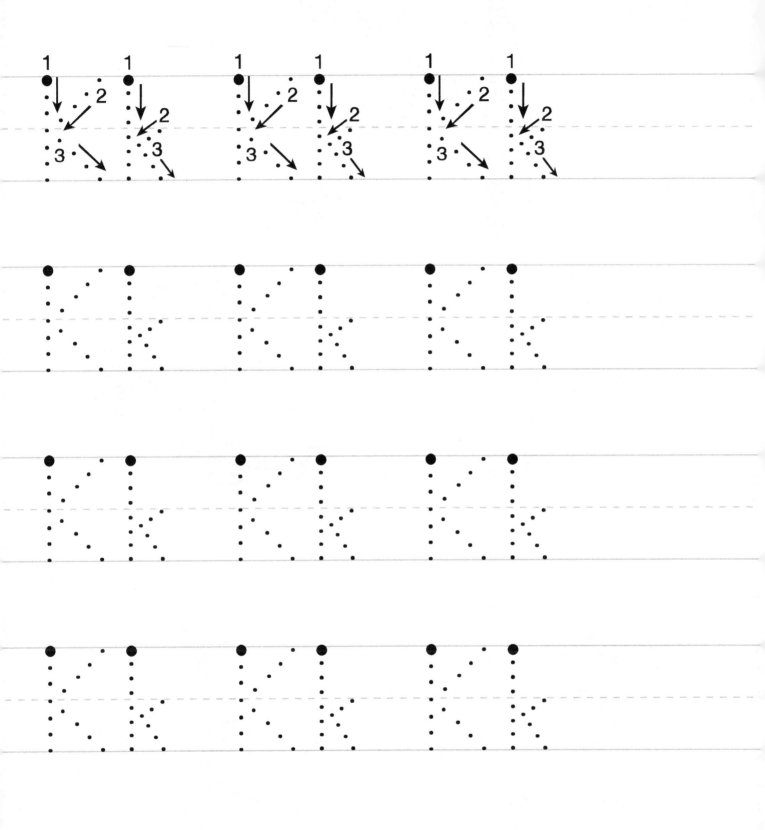

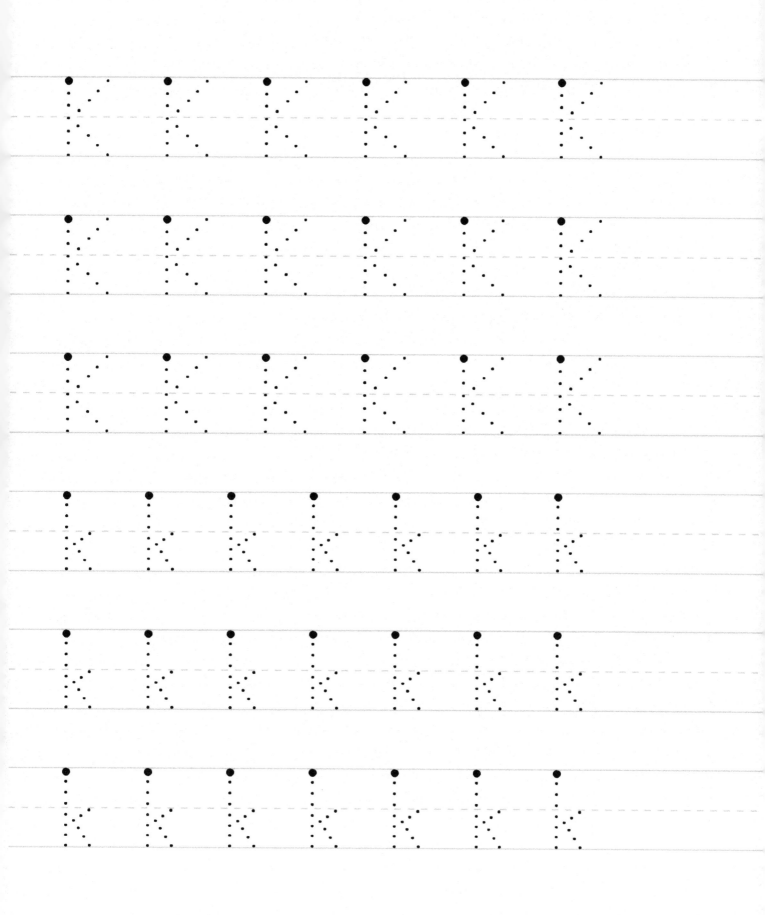

L

lamb

lion

lizard

ladder

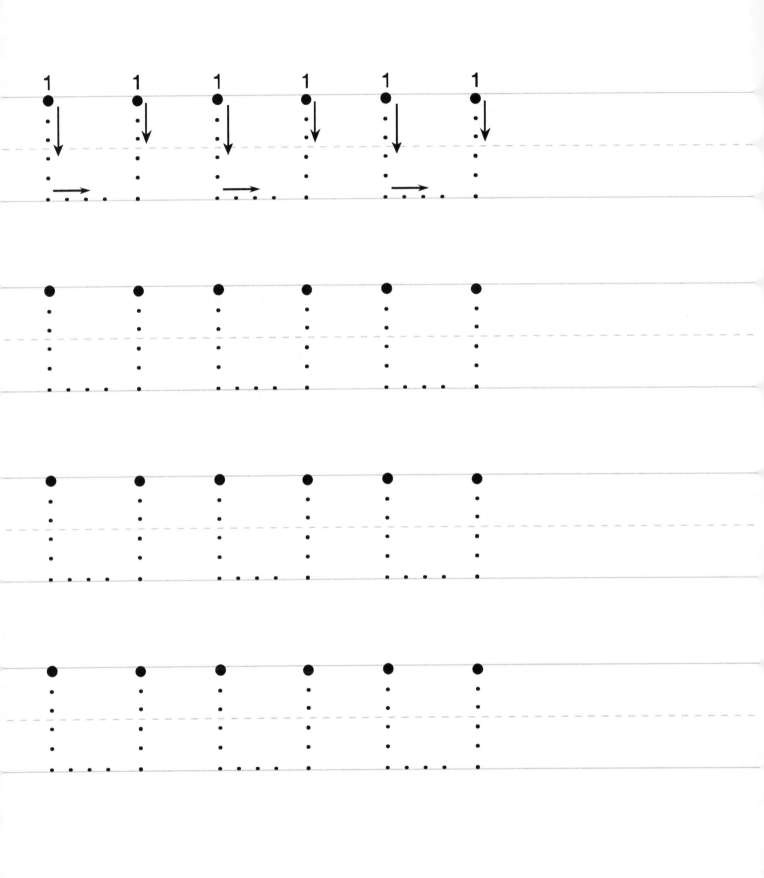

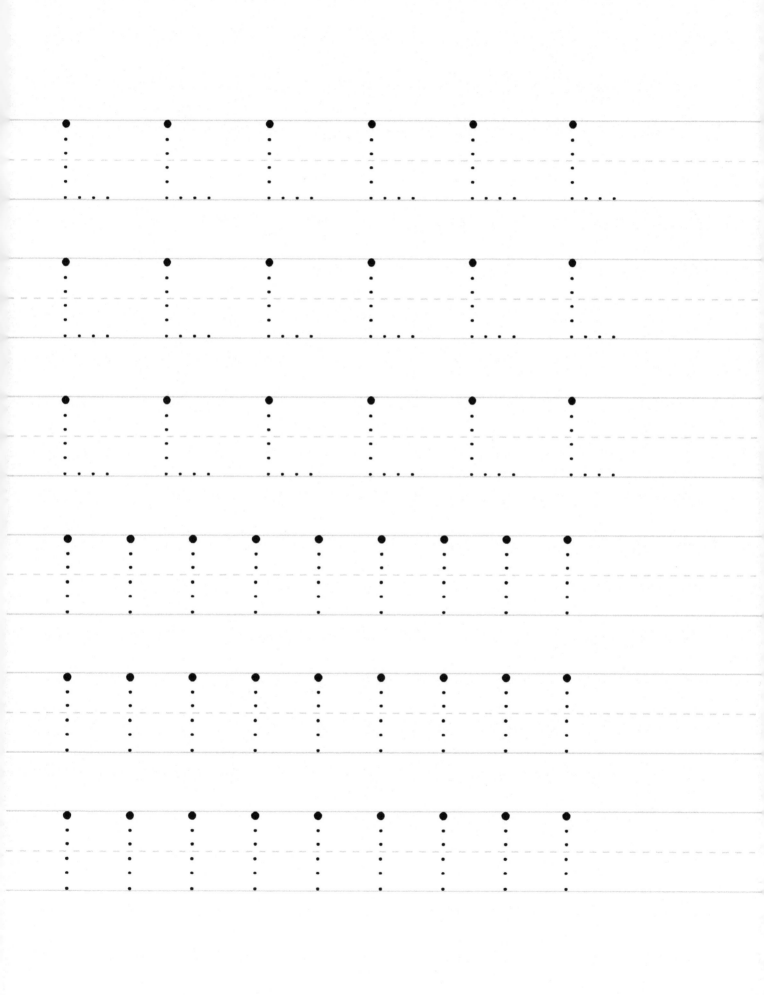

M

monkey

mouse

milk

mushroom

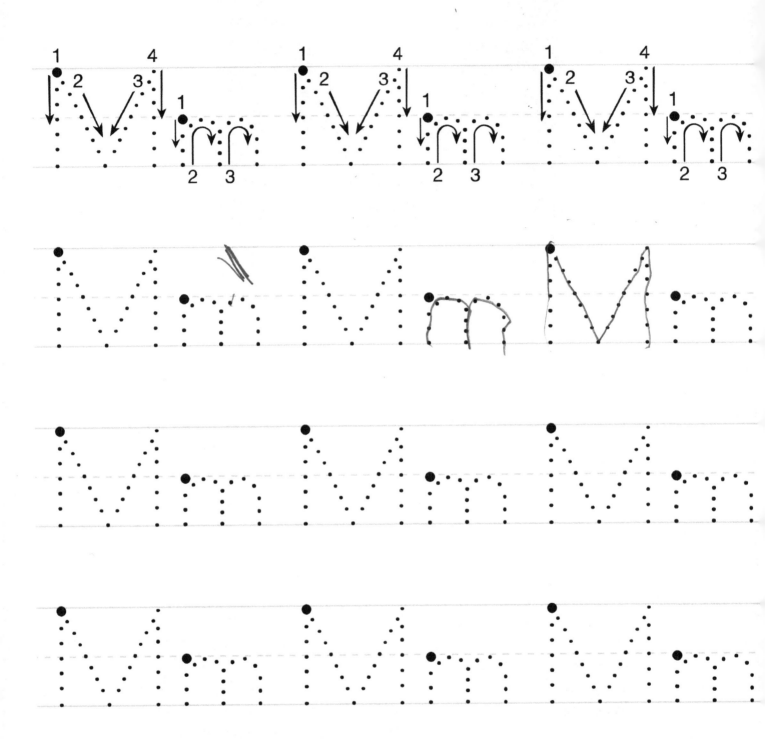

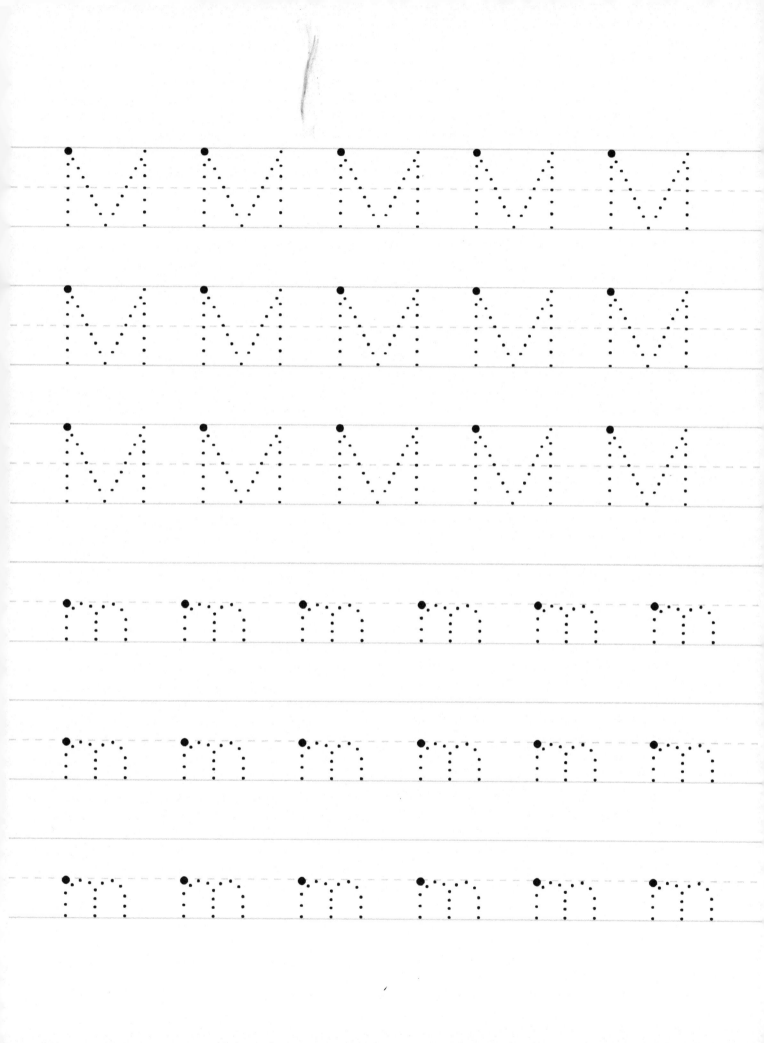

N

needle

nest

note

necktie

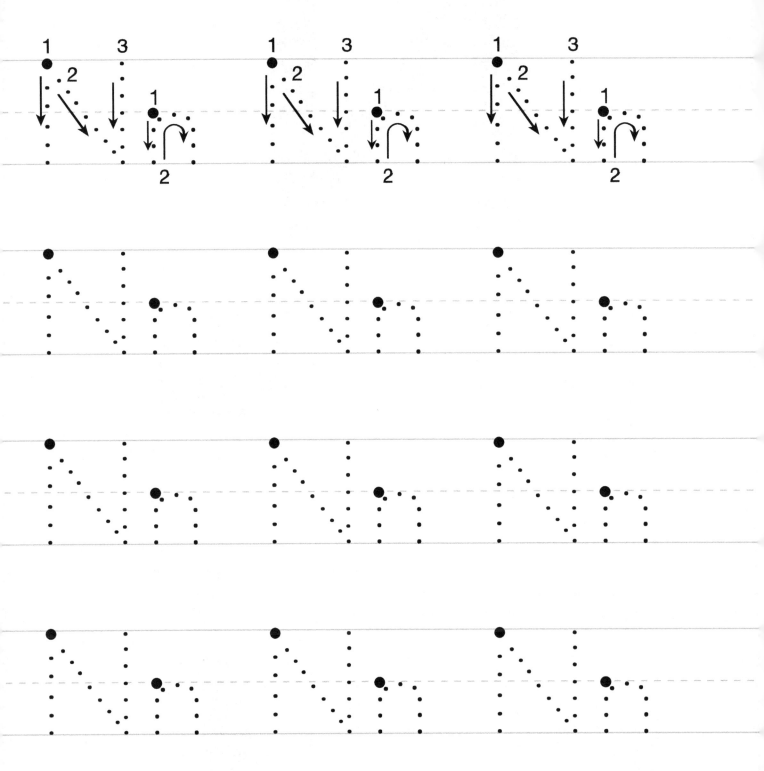

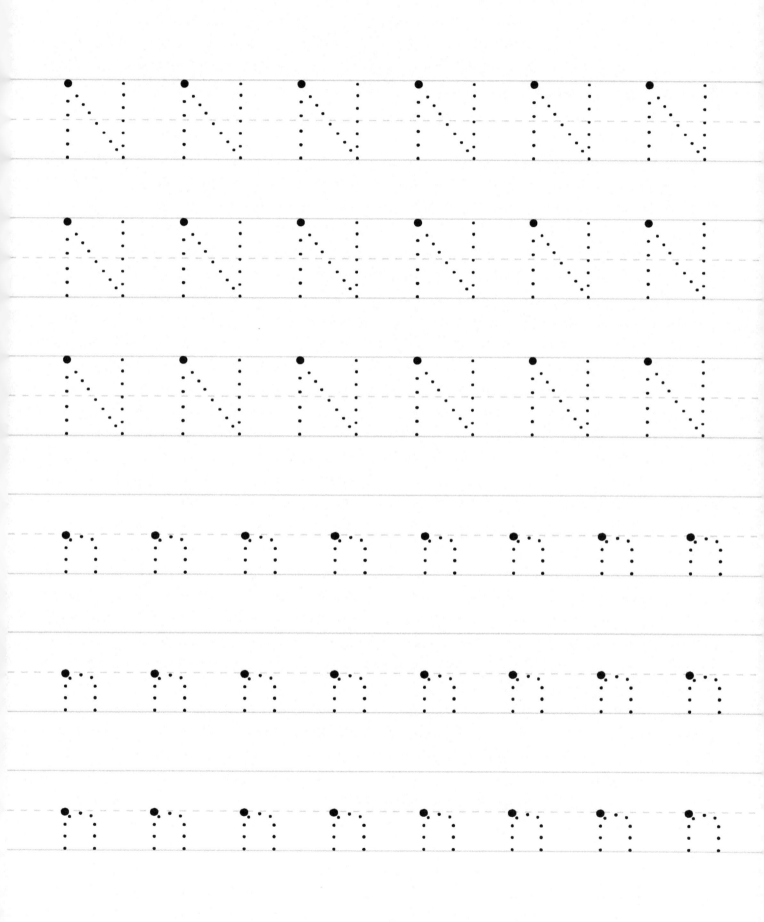

octopus

owl

ostrich

orange

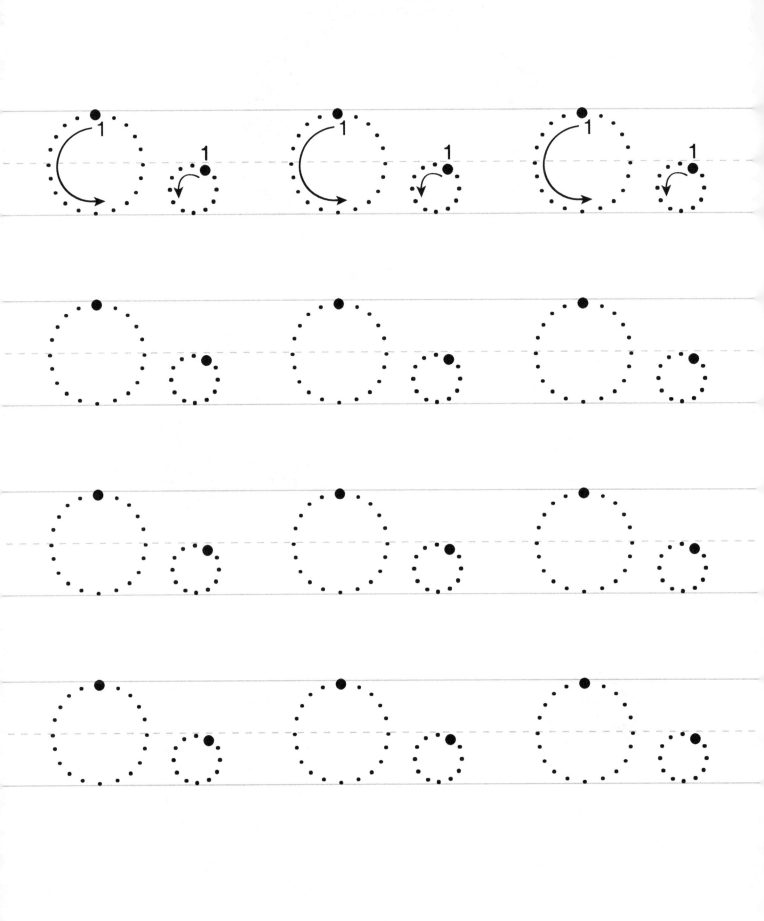

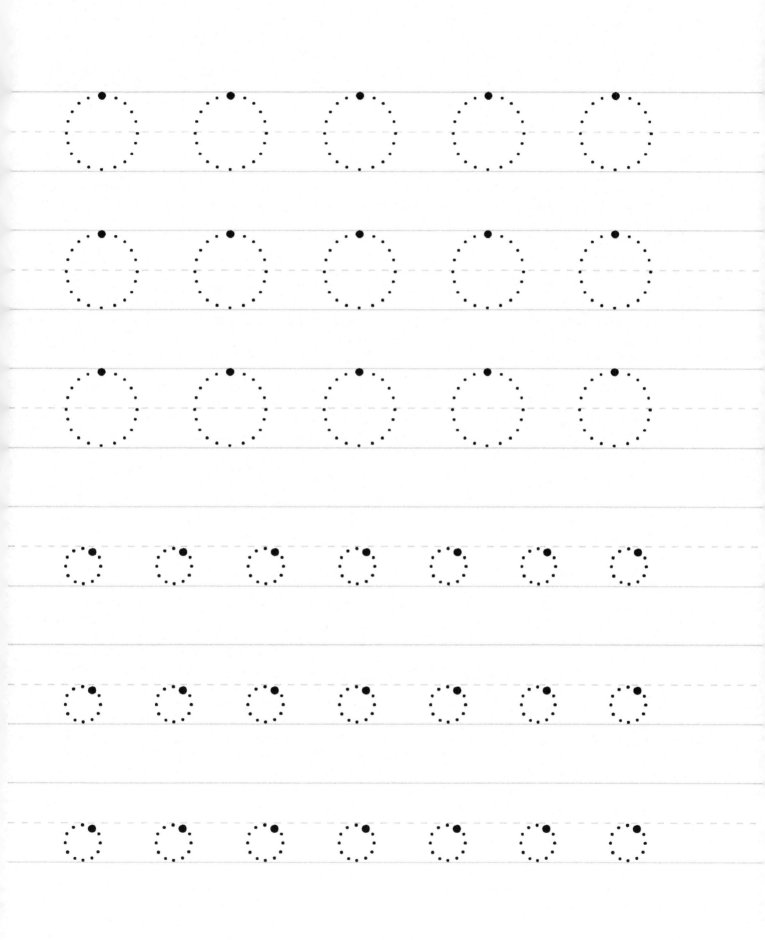

P

panda

pear

pencil

pig

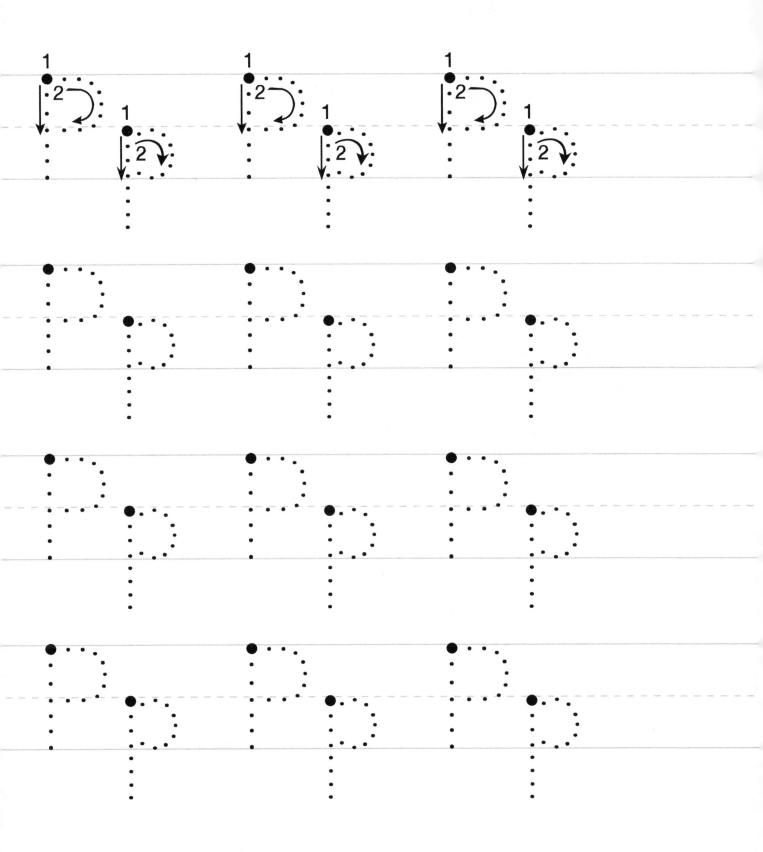

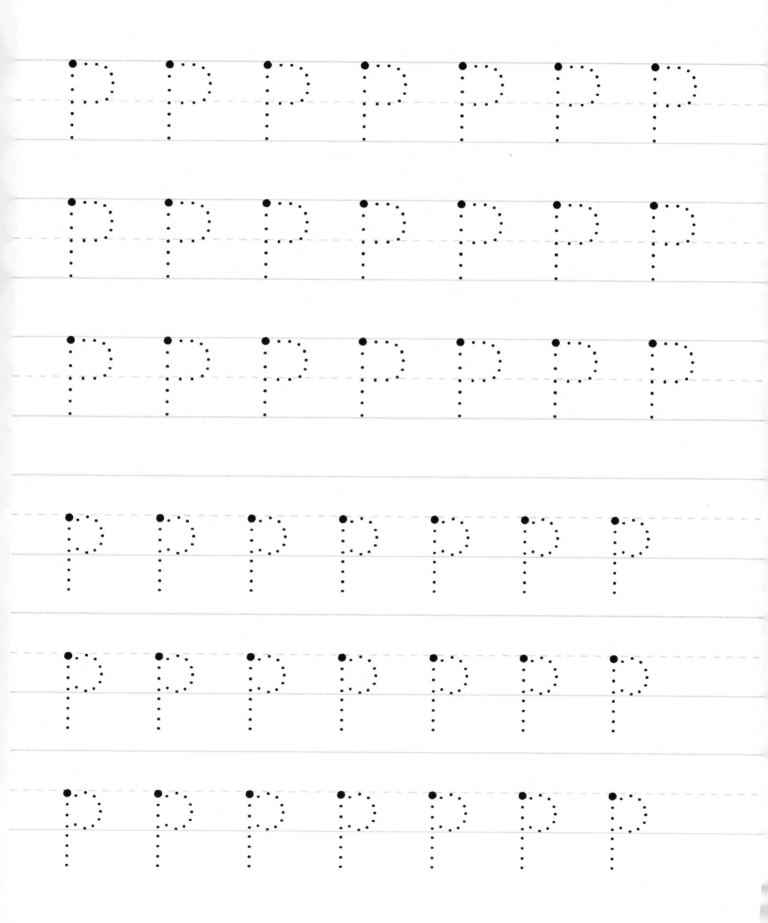

Q

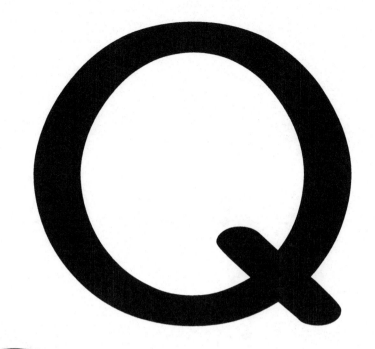

question

quilt

quarter

queen

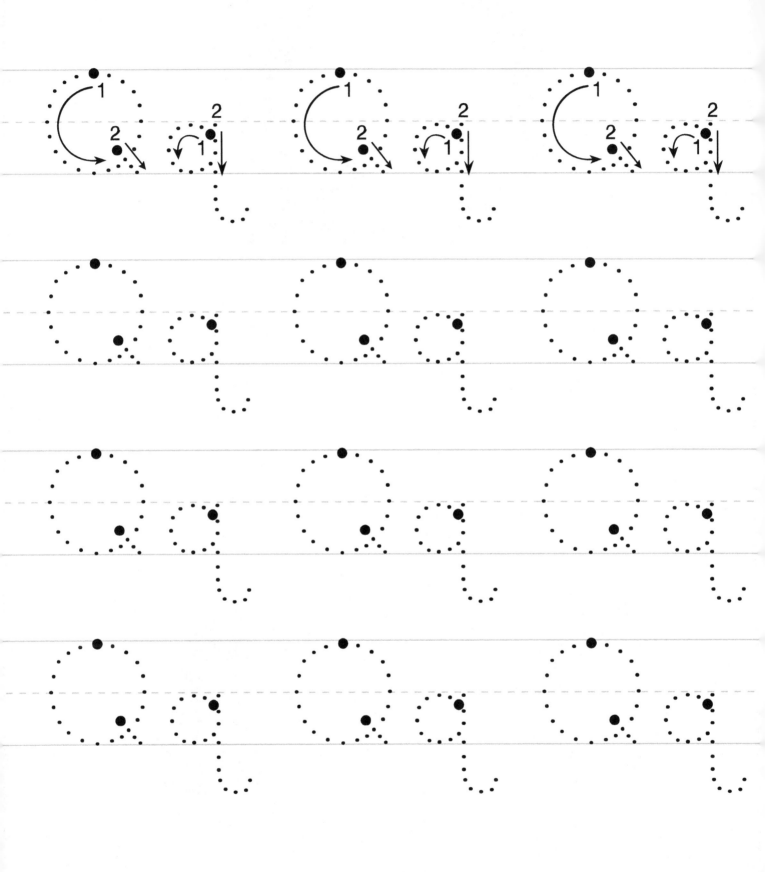

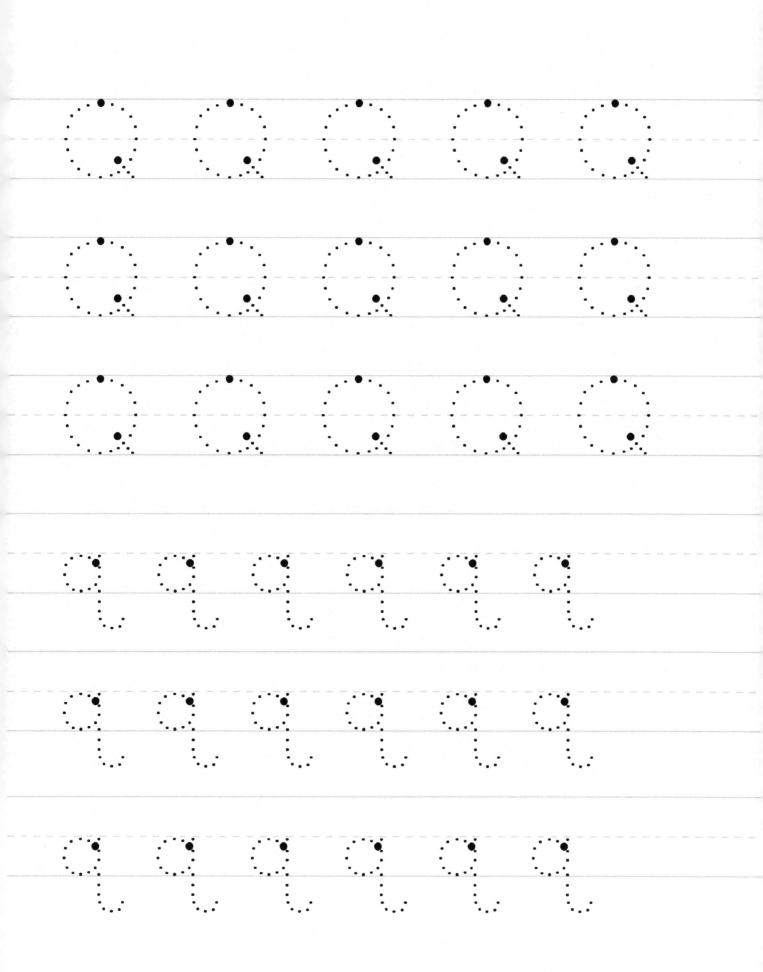

R

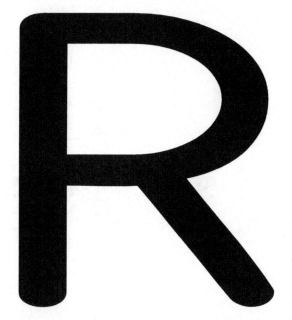

rooster

ring

rabbit

rose

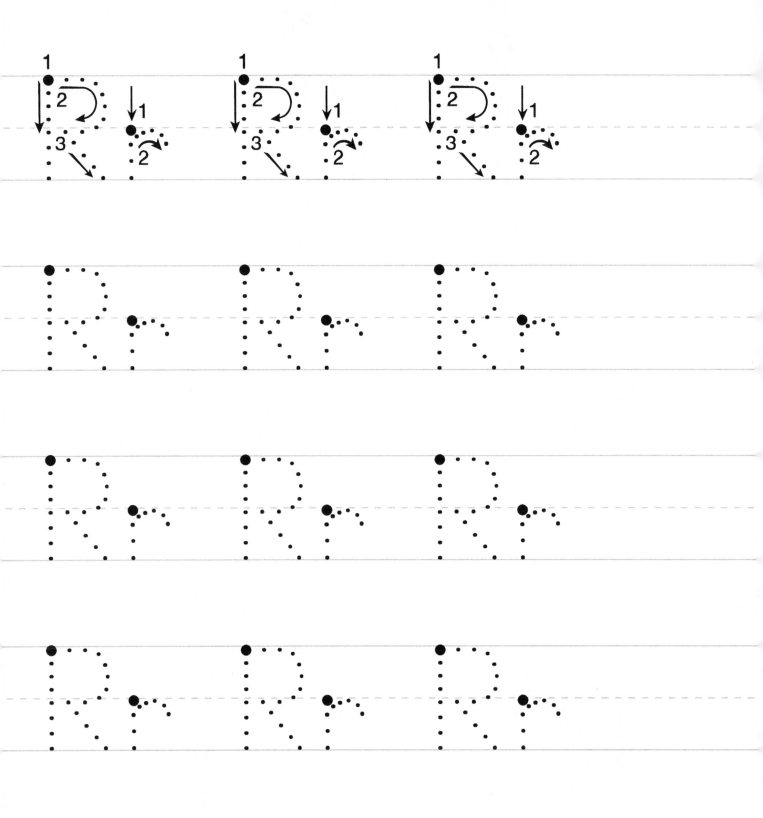

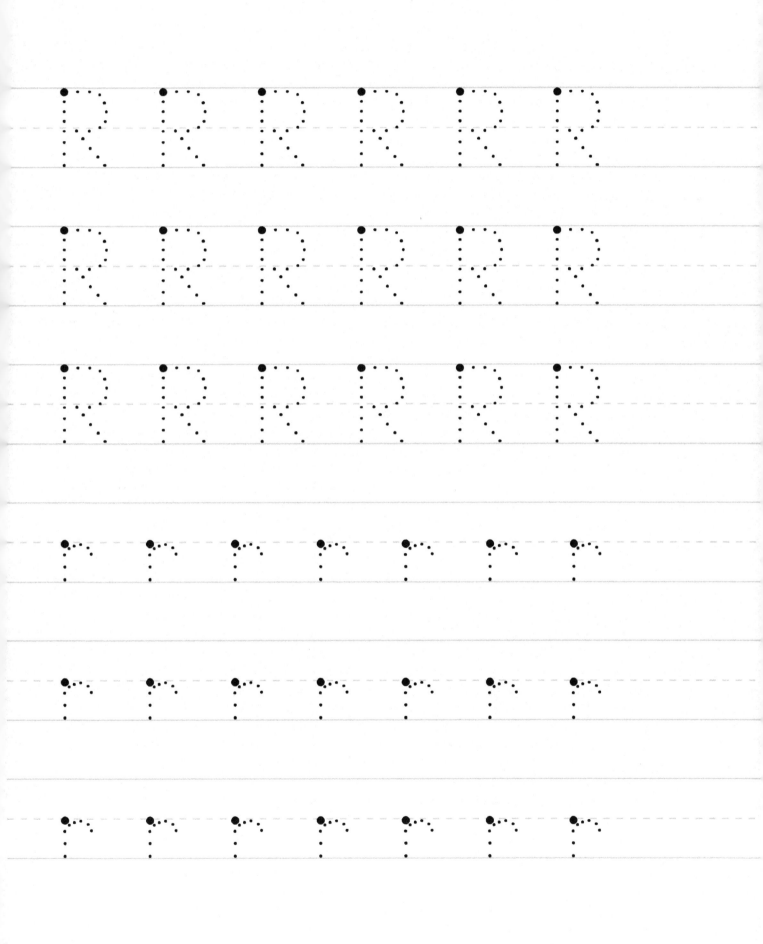

S

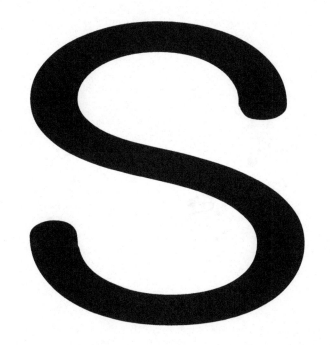

snake

socks

sun

sheep

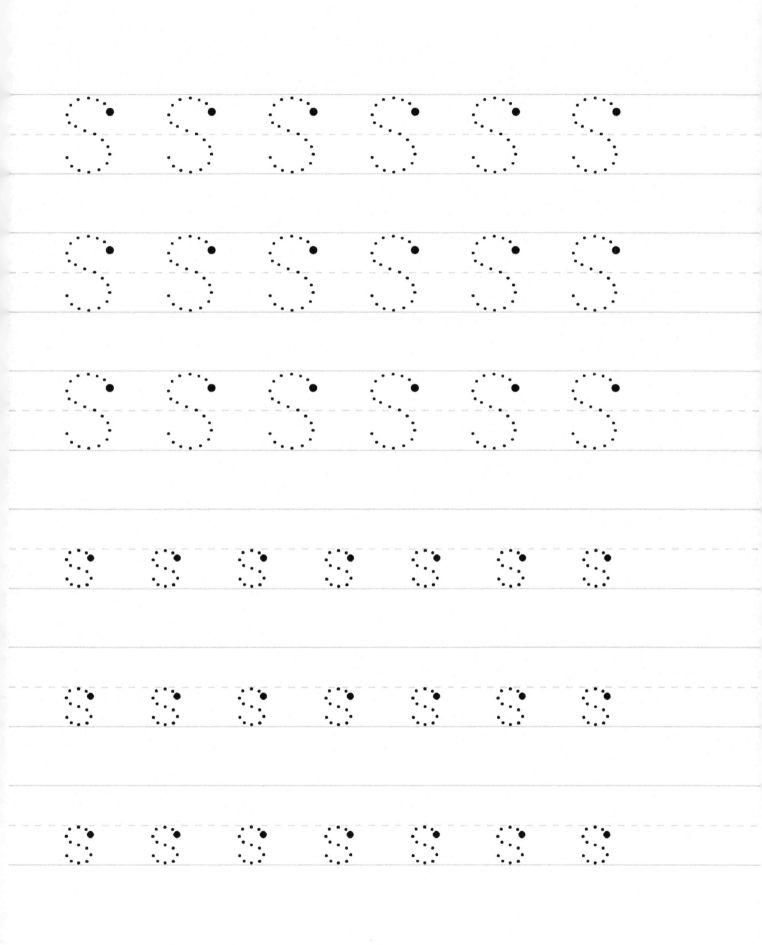

T

tomato

tiger

turtle

table

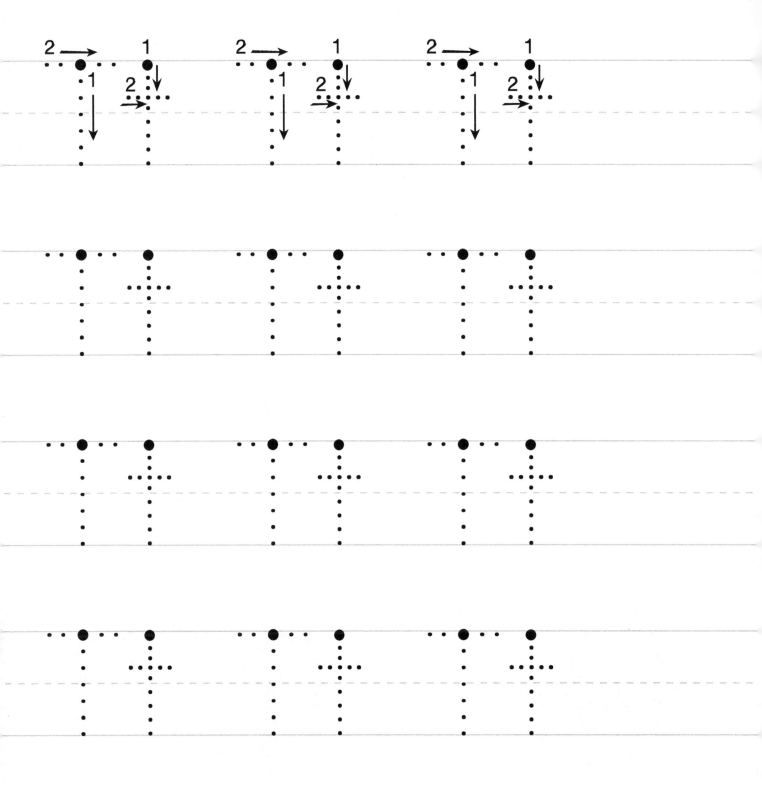

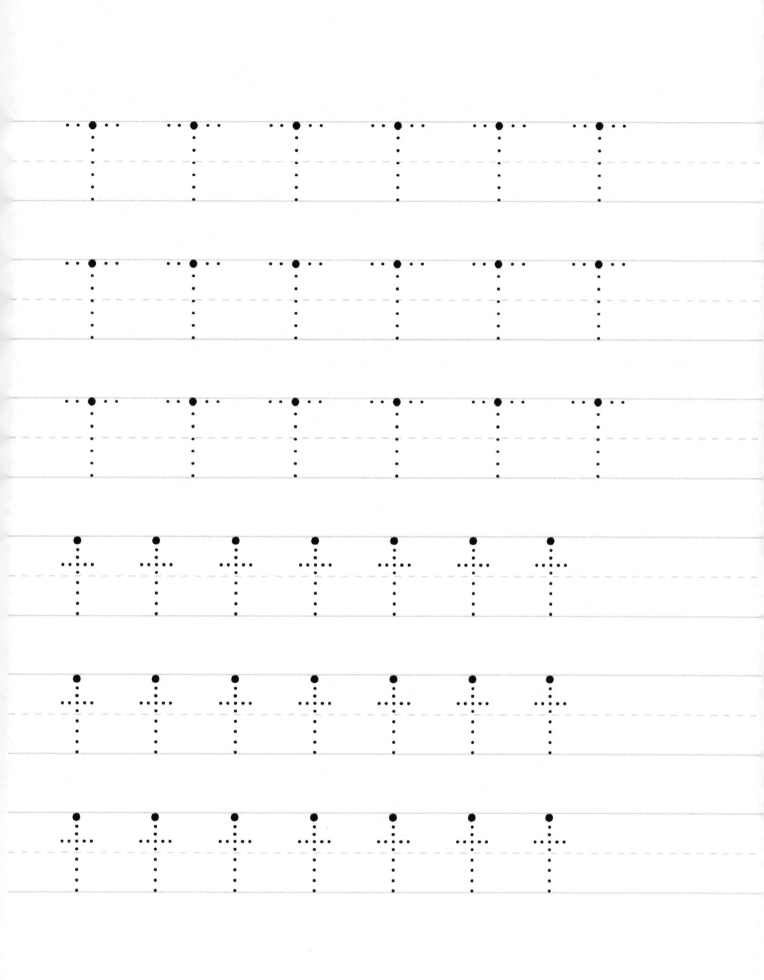

U

 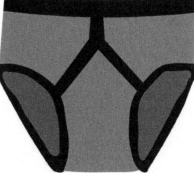

unicorn   underwear

unicycle   umbrella

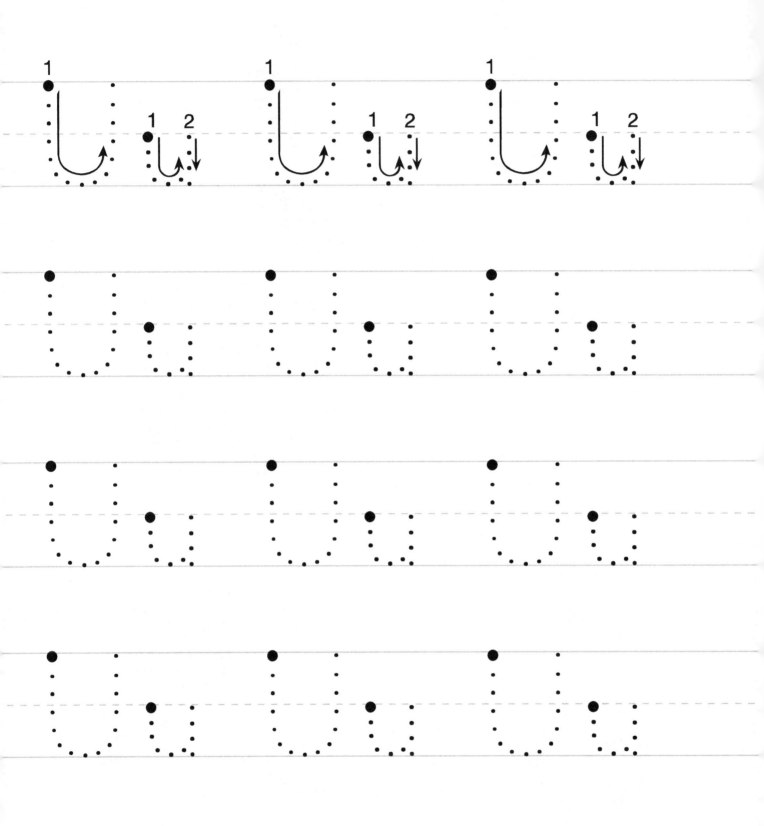

V

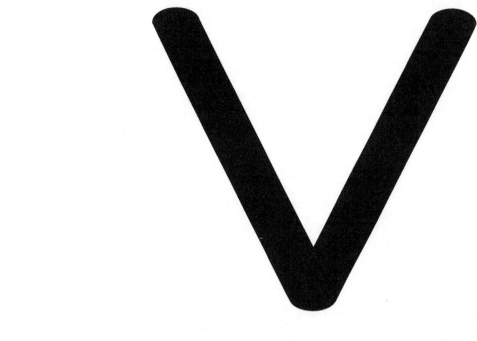

violin

vase

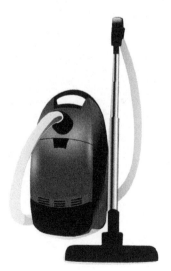

vacuum

van

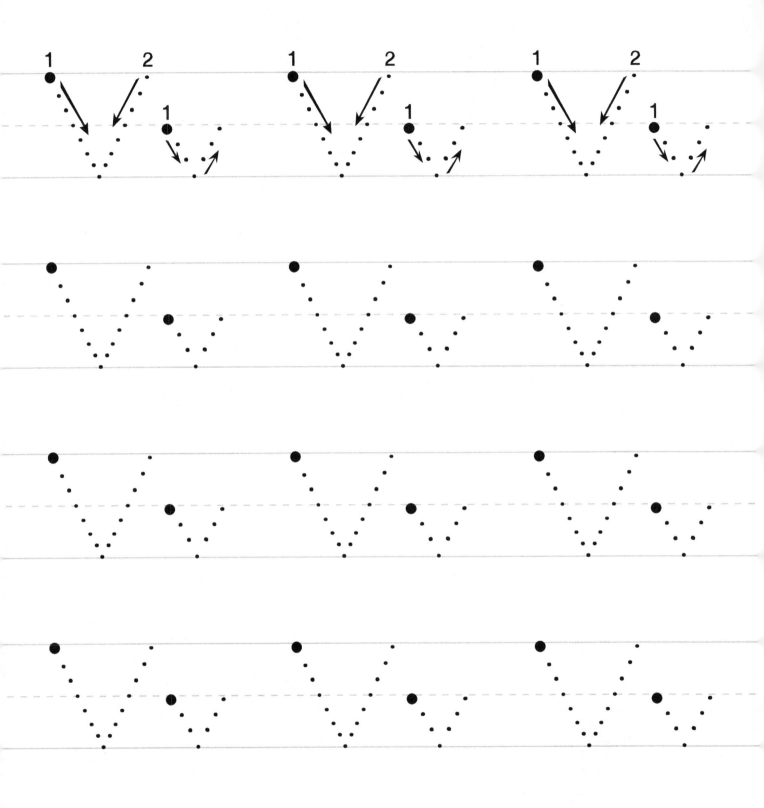

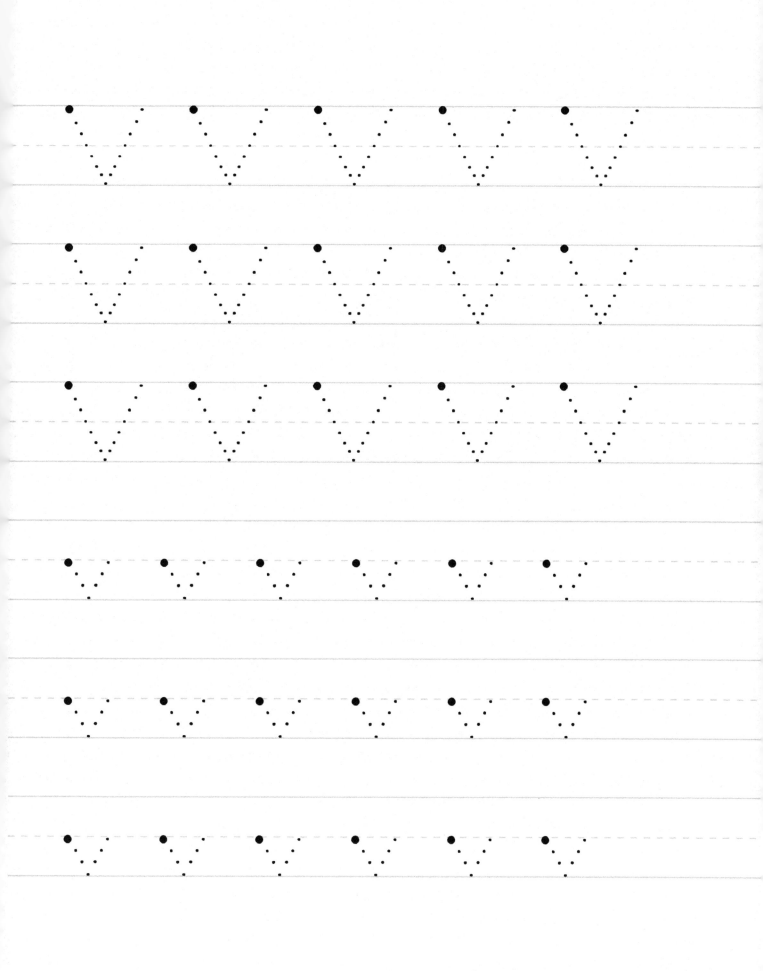

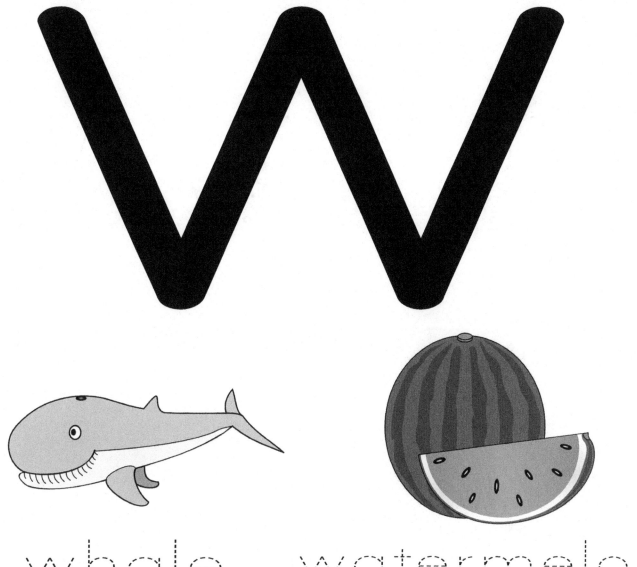

whale watermelon

window walrus

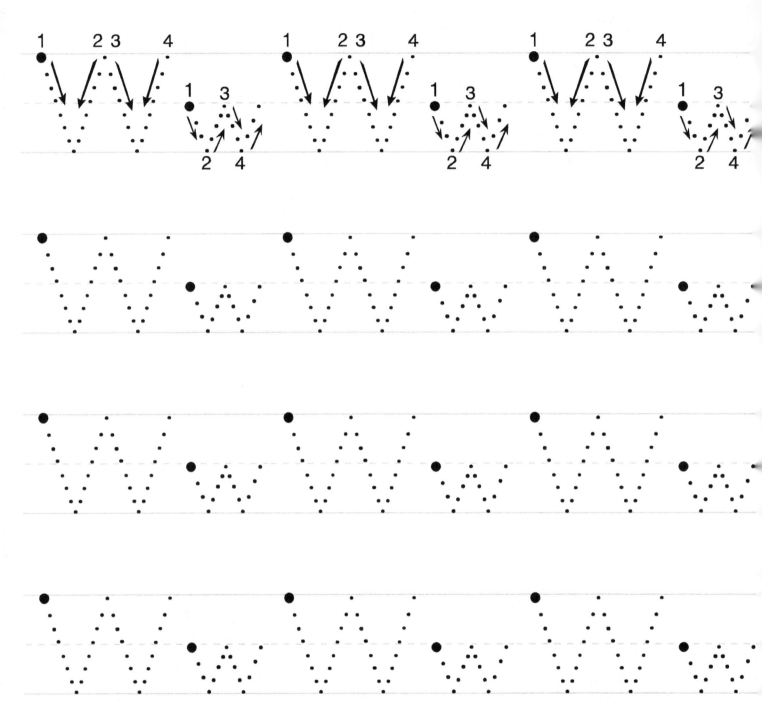

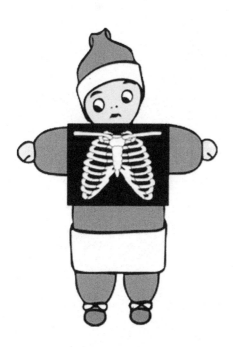

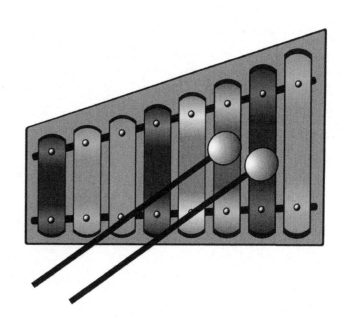

x-ray xylophone

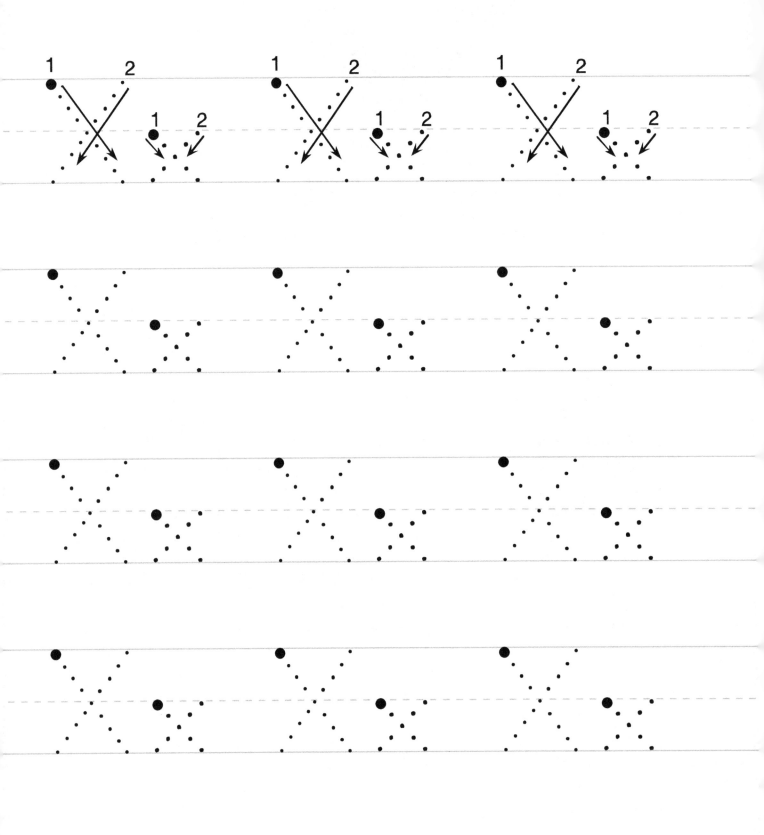

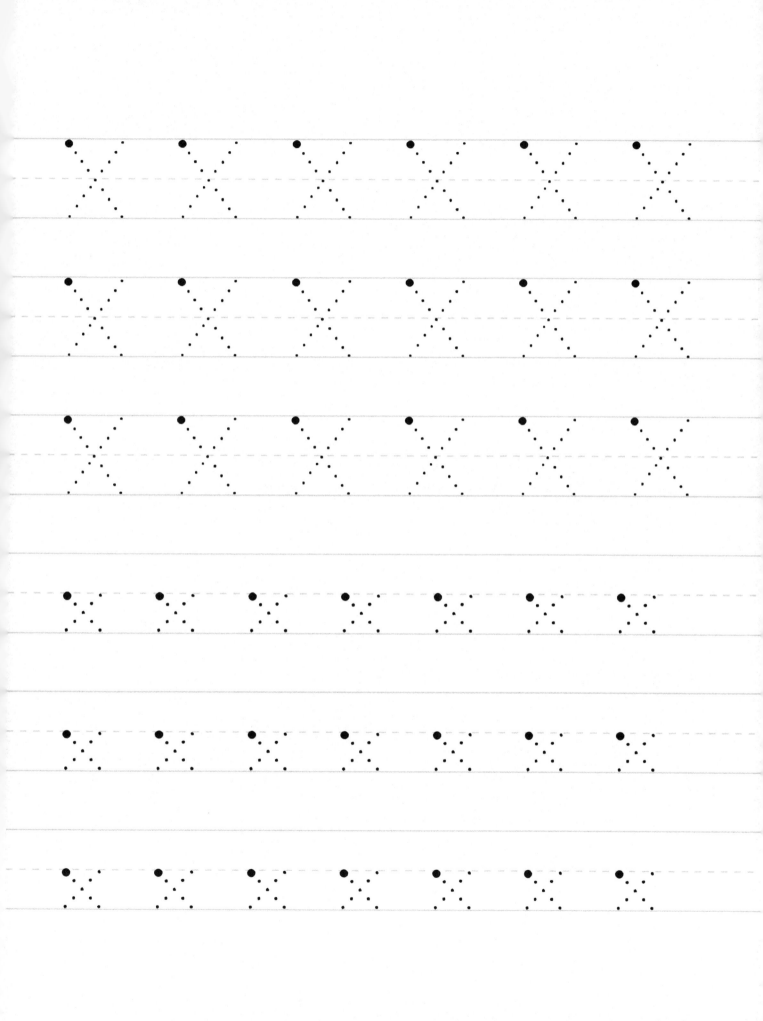

Y

yacht

yoyo

yarn

yak

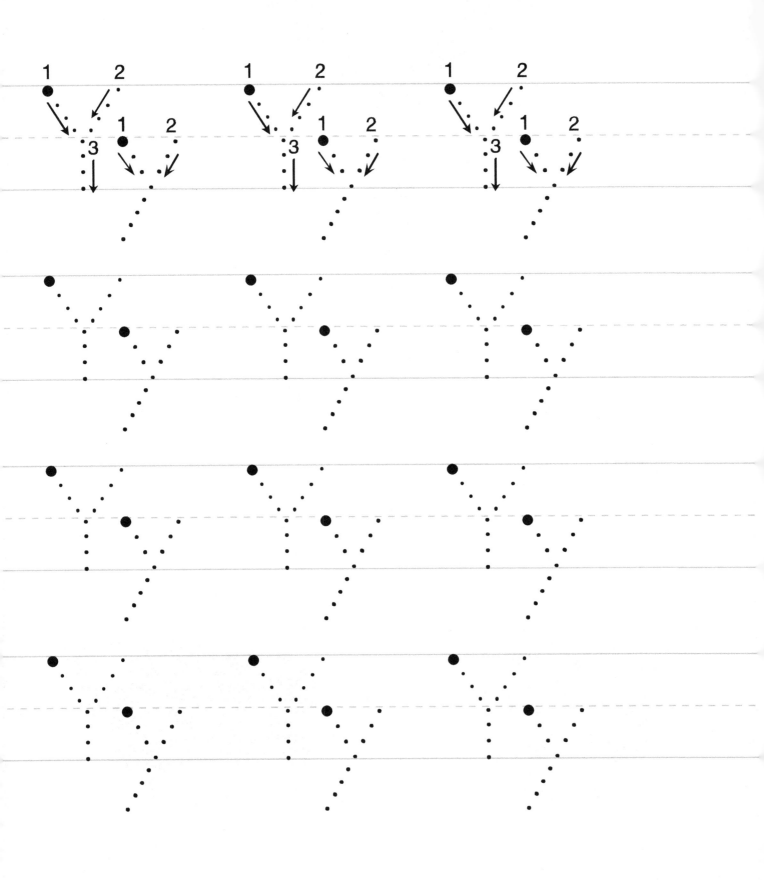

zipper

zucchini

zebra

zero

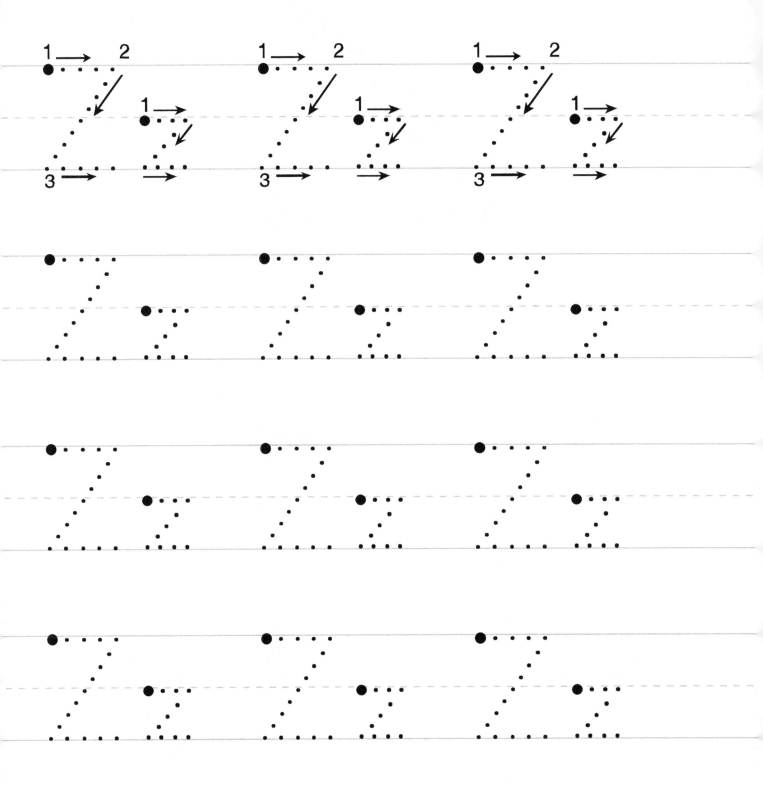

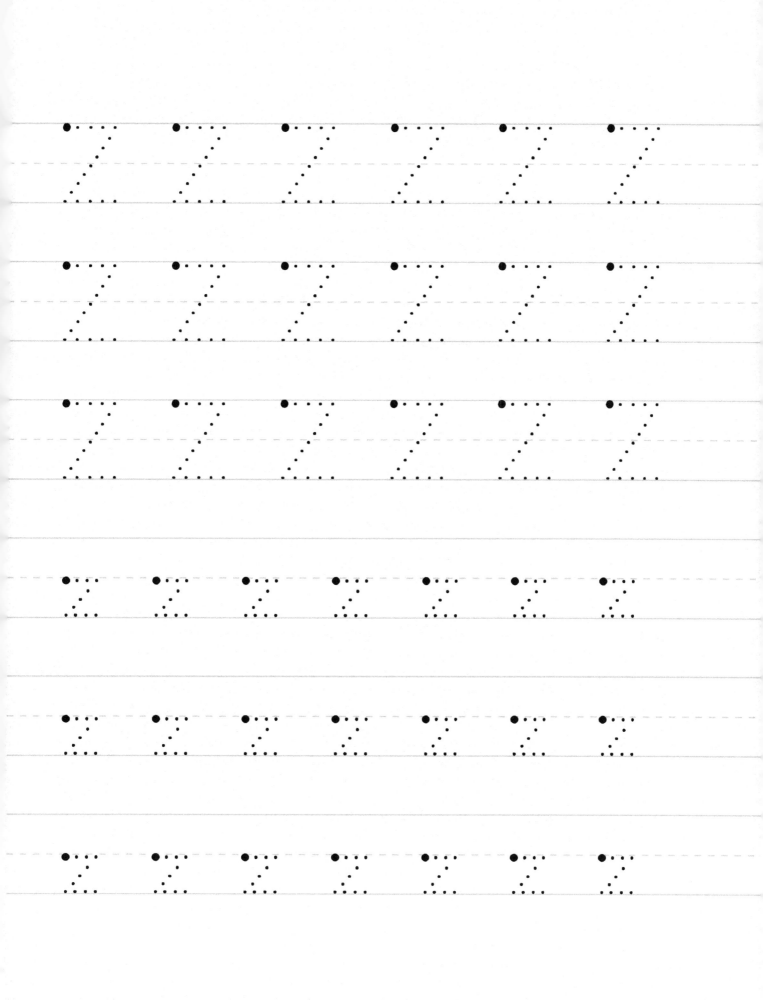

Made in the USA
Middletown, DE
09 November 2018